1918-2002

TED WILLIAMS: REMEMBERING THE SPLENDID SPLINTER
TED WILLIAMS: REMEMBERING THE SPLENDID SPLINTER

TED WILLIAMS
REMEMBERING THE
SPLENDID
SPLINTER

TED WILLIAMS: REMEMBERING THE SPLENDID SPLINTER
TED WILLIAMS: REMEMBERING THE SPLENDID SPLINTER

SPORTS PUBLISHING L.L.C.

www.SportsPublishingLLC.com

TED WILLIAMS: REMEMBERING THE SPLENDID SPLINTER
TED WILLIAMS: REMEMBERING THE SPLENDID SPLINTER

1918-2002

TED WILLIAMS
REMEMBERING THE
SPLENDID
SPLINTER

TED WILLIAMS: REMEMBERING THE SPLENDID SPLINTER
TED WILLIAMS: REMEMBERING THE SPLENDID SPLINTER

The Boston Herald

President and Publisher: **Patrick J. Purcell**

Editor: **Andrew F. Costello**

Executive Sports Editor: **Mark Torpey**

Director of Photography: **Garo Lachinian**

Vice President/Promotion: **Gwen Cage**

Chief Librarian: **John Cronin**

Sports Publishing L.L.C.

Publisher: **Peter L. Bannon**

Senior Managing Editors: **Susan M. Moyer**

and Joseph J. Bannon Jr.

Art Director: **K. Jeffrey Higgerson**

Graphic Designer: **Ralph Roether III**

Developmental Editor: **Erin Linden-Levy**

Copy Editor: **Cynthia L. McNew**

All stories and photographs are from the files of the *Boston Herald*

ISBN: 1-58261-586-1

www.SportsPublishingLLC.com

Contents

HE WAS LARGER THAN LIFE

THE 20TH CENTURY IS OFFICIALLY OVER

Steve Buckley

As Ted Williams was stepping to the plate for the last time on that chilly, gray weekday afternoon in 1960, Sen. John Fitzgerald Kennedy was in the final stages of his campaign for the presidency. It would be another 17 months before Ted's old Korean war buddy, Col. John Glenn, squeezed himself into Friendship 7 and became the first United States astronaut to orbit the earth. In Boston, Scollay Square was still a part of the urbanscape, though the wrecking ball was already performing its grim task.

Indeed, the world has changed so much, for better and for worse, in those 42 years since the Splendid Splinter's last at-bat. Yet we have never stopped talking about the man, have never stopped listing and cataloguing his many achievements, have never stopped comparing him with those squatty, flannel-encrusted players who came before him and those high-salaried stacks of beefcake who now patrol the game's green pastures. Ted Williams stopped playing, sure, but he was never an old baseball soldier who, MacArthur-like, simply faded away.

Ted Williams, 83 years old when he passed away Friday morning, remains as relevant now as he ever was. Crusty old-timers will tell you stories about the man's many exploits, but the beauty of Ted Williams — the magic of Ted Williams, a magic that will live on — is that today's teenagers can tell you many of those same stories, only without the I-was-there embellishment.

There has to be a reason for this, beyond the fact that Ted Williams was a great baseball player. Willie Mays, after all, is considered to be the greatest ALL-AROUND player in history. Henry Aaron eclipsed Babe Ruth's all-time home run record, and Mark McGwire, and then Barry Bonds, set new records for most home runs in a season.

Yet Ted Williams continued to capture our imagination in a way no other player had since Babe Ruth himself. And here's why: Just as the Babe seemed to define a distinct era in American history, so, too, did Theodore Samuel Williams define another era in American history.

Ted Williams was a Depression-era child who grew up to become entwined in two wars. He played baseball during the game's Golden Era, when players rode midnight trains from South Station to St. Louis. He was a modern-day Rough Rider: Just as Teddy Roosevelt disappeared into the Badlands to chase buffalo and break bread with roughnecks, Teddy Ballgame

SIGN OF THINGS TO COME: In 1939, rookie Ted Williams displays the batting swing that would make him the greatest hitter in baseball history.

PHOTO COURTESY OF THE ARTHUR GRIFFIN CENTER FOR PHOTOGRAPHIC ART, WINCHESTER

lobby of the Anaheim Marriott before Game 3 of the 1986 American League Championship Series between the Red Sox and California Angels, Williams started to rattle off the names of INTERNATIONAL LEAGUE players he had watched that season. He devoted five minutes alone to LaSchelle Tarver, a diminutive, opposite field-hitting outfielder whom Williams had seen that summer at Triple-A Pawtucket while hanging out with PawSox owner Ben Mondor.

Put it all together and what do you have? Ted Williams may have aged, but he never got old. He was as relevant in 2002 as he was when he broke into the big leagues in 1939. Not once did he ever pine for the good old days or make wisecracks about what he'd have done with today's journeyman meatball artists. In Ted Williams' view, the game was fine ... except that this was one oldtimey ballplayer with the gumption to admit it was high time the Red Sox ripped down Fenway Park.

And when he was inducted into the Hall of Fame in 1966, he dedicated his acceptance speech to the plight of the old, forgotten veterans of the Negro Leagues. Imagine: At a time when most baseball fans couldn't even name a Negro League ballplayer, beyond Satchel Paige and Josh Gibson, here was Ted Williams, on his grand day, asking that the gates to Cooperstown be swung open for those men who were excluded from the game for nearly half a century.

Now, add to all this the man's swagger, his sass, his I-can-lick-any-man-in-the-bar bravado, his unapologetic patriotism, and in many respects you have, as once was said about George M. Cohan, the entire nation squeezed into one pair of pants.

Put another way, Ted Williams WAS the 20th century. And now that he is gone, it is not an unreasonable suggestion that the 20th century is officially over.

disappeared into the Maine woods to go huntin' and fishin' with his pal Bud Leavitt. He was confidante to the likes of Ronald Reagan, George H.W. Bush and George W. Bush.

In his later years, at a time when he had every right to sit back in his rocking chair and spit venom at the modern-day game and its pricey players, Ted went the other way: He hunkered down and talked hitting with the likes of Tony Gwynn,

Wade Boggs and Don Mattingly. He was the first to point out that Paul Molitor's swing was not unlike Joe DiMaggio's. And even with his health failing, his vaunted eyesight going, he knew so much about Nomar Garciaparra's batting stance you'd swear he was locked away in a room, breaking down the videotape. And Williams didn't limit his critiques to the game's marquee attractions. During a chance meeting with Williams in the

Ted was baseball. Pure and simple. He had the picture-perfect swing and the best last at-bat of all time.

SPLINTER WAS SPLENDID WITH BLUNTNESS, CHARM

Karen Guregian

My first one-on-one contact with Ted Williams came in 1998, a week shy of his 80th birthday. During an August afternoon, we spoke on the phone. As it turned out, 20 minutes of shooting the breeze with Williams filled three days' worth of sports pages. It could have easily been more. That was Ted. Ask him a question, and you'd get an honest answer – and then some. There was no sugar-coating, no political correctness, and no apologies. Just rich and unadulterated candor.

Williams was direct and to the point. There was no gray area in his opinions. They were always black and white. You knew exactly where he stood. Naturally, that made for some wonderful copy. Here's a sample of The Kid's bluntness. During that conversation, I asked him what he thought about the potential of Mo Vaughn leaving the Red Sox. This is what he said: "He's a player, a very valuable player. He's established himself with the town and with the club. He shouldn't even be thinking about leaving Boston. In my mind, that would be a big, big, BIG mistake on his part."

Williams' view on Fenway Park was equally frank. He felt the fabled park on Yawkey Way should be dumped. Green Monster and all. It seems the legendary left fielder had no fondness for The Wall.

"I'm going to tell you straight off how I feel about it," Williams began. "There should be a new ballpark in Boston. I think Fenway Park has outlived its usefulness. I think a new park would stimulate the whole town. And the records prove without any question that a new park stimulates both the ballclub and the fans."

Whether his notions were right or wrong, popular or unpopular, Williams wasn't afraid to take a stand. He also wasn't shy about telling off someone he didn't like. Given that tidbit, I was somewhat apprehensive about speaking with the irascible icon for the first time. I was told Ted could be pretty tough on reporters, given his gruff and sometimes surly nature. Without question, his booming voice made you sit up at attention. Williams, however, was good-natured, humorous, even a bit self-deprecating during our conversation.

When I made mention of him being the greatest hitter who ever lived, he said with a laugh: "I guess I got you fooled. That's good."

On the occassion of his turning 80, Williams was naturally a bit nostalgic. When asked about his favorite lifetime memories, Teddy Ballgame pointed to baseball and his time in the service.

"I've been a very lucky guy and I know that," he said "but my greatest thanks is that I was able to do two things. One was that I was able to realize the career I had, and the great memories that go along with it. The other thing is I was a Marine. And I'm darn proud of that."

Was there anything he would have changed about his life, I asked? "Yeah," he answered. "Hit .400 two or three times." Like any baseball fan, Ted had his favorites with respect to players. He told me Ken Griffey Jr. was the left-handed hitter he most enjoyed watching while Nomar Garciaparra was his favorite from the right side.

"Anybody that gets a chance to see Garciaparra play, they can just say I'm watching one of the greatest players that might ever be in this game," Williams said. "He's a great kid, and boy, I'll tell you, I don't know of anyone I'd rather watch than Garciaparra hit a baseball."

Coming from the greatest hitter who ever lived, that was some compliment. It's like Luciano Pavarotti singling out a young opera star and saying there was no one he'd rather hear sing an aria. Ted was baseball. Pure and simple. He had the picture-perfect swing and the best last at-bat of all time.

During the All-Star game at Fenway Park in 1999, I remember actor Kevin Costner speaking about Williams, speaking of him as being a real-life god, someone to be revered and treasured.

Only now, he's gone. The Splendid Splinter has left us. Gods, however, aren't ever forgotten. They stick around in our hearts and minds. I just know for one day, I was lucky enough to get 20 minutes of non-stop Ted. And much like his every at-bat, it turned out to be a blast.

DAWN OF A LEGENDARY CAREER: Ted Williams peers into the sunshine during his rookie season, 1939.
PHOTO COURTESY OF THE ARTHUR GRIFFIN CENTER FOR PHOTOGRAPHIC ART, WINCHESTER

THE KING OF SWING

AS A HITTER, TED WILLIAMS WAS THE BEST

David Cataneo

After the pregame workout, they were hot and dusty and the flannel stuck to their sweaty backs, but they lingered before retreating into the clubhouse for a cold drink. In the 1940s and '50s, opposing ballplayers were as curious and impressed as 10-year-old boys when the Red Sox took batting practice. "The other players? They'd stay on the bench to watch Ted hit," Matt Batts once said. The old catcher was reminiscing about his one-time Red Sox teammate, Ted Williams. "Everybody loved to watch him hit."

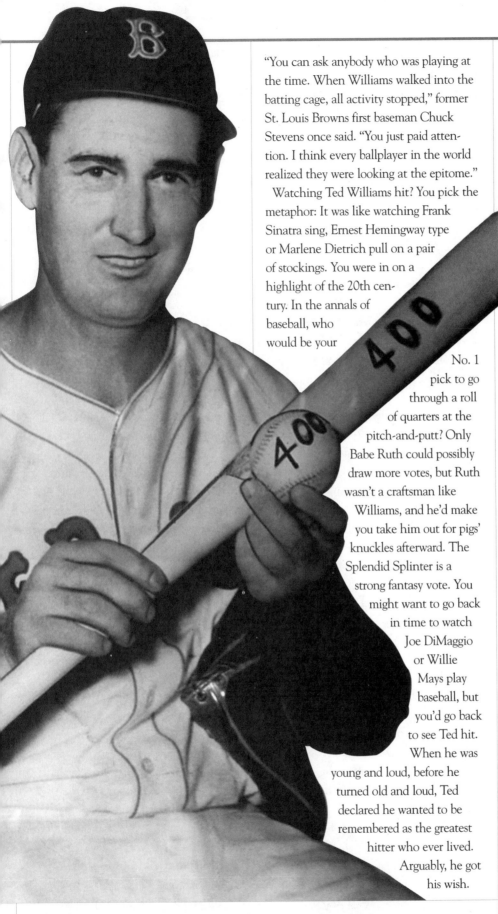

"You can ask anybody who was playing at the time. When Williams walked into the batting cage, all activity stopped," former St. Louis Browns first baseman Chuck Stevens once said. "You just paid attention. I think every ballplayer in the world realized they were looking at the epitome."

Watching Ted Williams hit? You pick the metaphor: It was like watching Frank Sinatra sing, Ernest Hemingway type or Marlene Dietrich pull on a pair of stockings. You were in on a highlight of the 20th century. In the annals of baseball, who would be your No. 1 pick to go through a roll of quarters at the pitch-and-putt? Only Babe Ruth could possibly draw more votes, but Ruth wasn't a craftsman like Williams, and he'd make you take him out for pigs' knuckles afterward. The Splendid Splinter is a strong fantasy vote. You might want to go back in time to watch Joe DiMaggio or Willie Mays play baseball, but you'd go back to see Ted hit. When he was young and loud, before he turned old and loud, Ted declared he wanted to be remembered as the greatest hitter who ever lived. Arguably, he got his wish.

Ted Williams holding bat and ball marked with his 400 record.
PHOTO COURTESY OF NEW ENGLAND SPORTS MUSEUM

He hit .344 lifetime with 521 home runs. The greatest hitter who ever lived? A lot of old-timers say he was the best they laid eyes on.

"I can't say Ted was the greatest hitter who ever lived, because there were some great hitters who I did not see," DiMaggio once said. "Like Ruth (.342, 714 home runs), Ty Cobb (.366, 117), Rogers Hornsby (.358, 301) and George Sisler (.340, 102). But from 1936 to the present day, I can't say I've seen a better hitter than Ted Williams."

"I always hate to call him the greatest hitter I ever saw," former Tigers and Red Sox catcher Birdie Tebbetts once said. "But he was."

Late in life, when brashness had worn off, the once-cocky Kid made a stunning pronouncement.

"I really, in my heart, never, never thought I was the greatest hitter who ever played the game," Williams said in the early 1990s. "Whenever I go to banquet and they want to announce me as the greatest hitter who ever lived, I want to get down off the chair and hide. I really do."

He can't hide in the history books.

Williams is sixth all-time in batting average, tied for 11th in home runs, eighth in home run percentage and 12th in RBIs.

Williams is second behind Ruth in slugging percentage (.634 to .690) and third in walks (2,019) behind Rickey Henderson (2,060) and Ruth (2,056), but he struck out far less than the Babe (709 to 1,330).

Something else, though, is beyond argument: No one studied, scrutinized, analyzed, practiced and loved hitting more than Williams. He said hitting a baseball was the hardest feat in sports.

Some people endlessly tidy their apartments. Williams endlessly studied his swing.

"He could be compulsive," said Tebbetts, Williams' roommate from 1947-50.

"You can ask anyone who was playing at the time. When Williams walked into the batting cage all activity stopped."

CHUCK STEVENS. FORMER ST. LOUIS BROWNS FIRST BASEMAN

This meant rolling out bed in the middle of the night to take imaginary cuts. Or rolling a restaurant menu into an imaginary bat to demonstrate proper wrist action. Or driving down to the ballpark early to get somebody — anybody — to pitch to him, so he could work on something only he could see.

"It never left his mind," Tebbetts said. "If I could hit like him, I wouldn't have thought about anything else, either." It also meant talking about hitting anywhere, any time, to anybody who would listen, which usually meant anybody within earshot. Williams talked hitting with Ruth, Hornsby, Cobb, Joe Cronin, Lefty O'Doul and Jimmy Foxx.

He talked hitting with Matt Batts.

"He'd discuss hitting with any player," Batts said. "There wasn't anything he didn't know about hitting. He'd talk with a group, three or four guys. He'd talk one-on-one. If there was something you wanted to know, he'd show you.

"I can still picture him up there shadow swinging. Sometimes he would have a bat in his hands. He would stand up and go through the motions of hitting. I can still see him up there in front of the lockers, showing the fellows how to hit. When other players came into Boston, they'd ask him for help, and he'd be glad to do it. He loved to do it."

Tebbetts said: "I have a picture here that I'm putting on my wall. It says, 'Birdie, I was your hitting coach. Signed, Ted Williams.' If he saw something that could help you, he made sure he got around to telling you about it."

Williams called his book *The Science of Hitting*, but he approached it like an art. Other than advocating the use of a light bat and the customary mechanics, with an emphasis on hips and wrists, he hated to tinker with individual swings. He detested set styles such as the Charley Lau-Walter Hriniak method. When he was shooting the breeze with his teammates or working with his players when he managed the Washington Senators or helping young Red Sox players as a spring training instructor, he preached comfort at the plate, concentration and intelligence.

"In my 22 years of professional baseball, I went to bat almost 8,000 times," he wrote in the 1970 batting bible, "and every trip to the plate was an adventure, one that I could remember and store up as information. I honestly believe I can recall everything there was to know about my first 300 home runs. Who the pitcher was, the count, the pitch itself, where the ball landed."

It helped. In the 1949 All-Star Game at Ebbets Field, Giants right-hander Larry Jansen threw Williams two slow curves. He fouled off both of them. Then Jansen threw a fastball inside, and Williams took it for a called third strike.

Cleveland manager Lou Boudreau was watching and later instructed his pitcher, Jim Bagby, how to work on Williams. Next time in Boston, Bagby started against Williams with a pair of slow curves, just like Jansen. Williams fouled off both.

Then Bagby fired a fastball inside, just like Jansen. Williams smacked it into the seats.

"Ted was the kind of guy who could have hit against a pitcher in 1941," Stevens once said, "and in 1943, he could remember the pitching sequence that guy used on him."

Williams, who declared hitting at least 50 percent mental, made sure he could step to the plate without distractions. He made sure his bats were clean, his cap not too tight, his pants not too baggy, his uniform sleeves not flappy. He kept the label of his bat turned away so he wouldn't see it flash by as he swung. Williams was all business at the plate, which wasn't easy in the days when catchers did everything but put on a cocktail dress to rattle a hitter.

"That's the way I made a living, trying to distract hitters," said Tebbetts, who, as a catcher with the Tigers, played against Williams for parts of eight seasons. "But you couldn't distract him. He was intense. Every great hitter was intense.

"There was only one guy I saw shake up Ted Williams, and that was Jake Early. He was a catcher for the Senators. He did a perfect imitation of a tobacco auctioneer, at the time when auctions were popular. When Williams would get up, Jake Early would auction off a brand of tobacco. Finally, Ted would have to stop the game, call time out and bust up laughing. He did it about once every series. We all waited for him to do it."

Williams had great eyesight, strong wrists and intense concentration. But one of the reasons Ted Williams was perhaps the greatest hitter who ever lived was because he wanted to be. "He wanted to do everything," Tebbetts said. "Have you got a pencil? OK. He wanted to lead the league in batting average. He wanted to lead the league in base on balls. He wanted

THE KING OF SWING:
Ted Williams warms up
and takes a swing.

PHOTO COURTESY OF
NEW ENGLAND SPORTS MUSEUM

to lead the league in home runs. He wanted to lead the league in RBIs. He wanted to lead the league in [fewest] strikeouts.

"He wanted to lead the league in everything. And I really believe, at any time during a game, he know exactly where he stood in all those categories."

Ted Williams thought hitting was the greatest challenge in sports, and his compulsive, grouchy, contrary personality loved to stuff a challenge.

"One time, we went into Chicago to play a series," Tebbetts said. "He was about three points behind Boudreau. I said to him before a doubleheader, 'The Frenchman's got you,' and walked away.

"In the first game, he got 3 for 4. The fifth time up, he turned to me and said, 'This one's for Ted.' And he hit a home run. He looked at me after the game and just grinned."

Fans, ballplayers and other strangers loved to watch him do that sort of thing. When they watched Williams at the plate, they knew they were in on something special.

Tebbetts was told that there are a lot of people too young to have ever seen Ted Williams hit a baseball.

"You missed something," he said.

1941

YEAR OF MEMORABLE FEATS: TED'S .406, JOE D.'S 56

Michael Gee

It is the single greatest and most celebrated accomplishment in the career of one of baseball's greatest and most famous players. And yet, for all its fame, Ted Williams' .406 batting average for the 1941 season has always been an underappreciated feat. Williams never got the proper credit for being the last man to hit .400, because he did so the year Joe DiMaggio hit in 56 consecutive games.

Mention 1941 to a baseball fan and their first reaction likely will be "DiMaggio's streak." Ask that same fan to say which of the game's records will never be broken, and he or she will surely answer, "Nobody will ever touch DiMaggio's 56-game hitting streak."

What is true today was true back in 1941. DiMaggio's streak captivated the country. It was the stuff of daily sports headlines and a Tin Pan Alley novelty hit. Williams' season-long battle to hit .400 attracted abiding interest only in New England.

DiMaggio, not Williams, was voted the American League's MVP for 1941, even though Williams' numbers were superior (.406, a league-leading 37 homers and 120 RBIs to DiMaggio's .357, 30 and 125). That may be attributable to the fact the Yankees won the pennant, finishing 17 games up on the second-place Sox.

New York had a far more dominant place in American culture in 1941 than it does today, and the Yankees, as the premier franchise in sports, reflected that. The Yanks were the original America's Team, followed by the huge parts of the country that had no big-league team for which to root. A Yankee who did something memorable would naturally get more attention than a Red Sox player (or Indian or Cardinal) who did so.

Most of all, DiMaggio got credit for making history because the baseball audience of 1941 was more aware of his hitting streak history. DiMaggio challenged, broke and shattered the 44-game record set by Wee Willie Keeler in 1897 during the dead-ball era. Fans knew the game had changed immeasurably since then, that what DiMaggio was doing was special.

By contrast, Williams' successful quest to hit .400 was exceptional, but it wasn't unique. In the 20th century, batters had hit .400 or better nine times.

The accomplishment wasn't shrouded in the mists of time, either. Bill Terry of the Giants was the last man to top the mark, hitting .401 in 1930, only 11 years earlier.

JUST WARMING UP: Ted Williams takes a practice cut during the Sox' first visit to Yankee Stadium in April 1941. He was limited to one pinch-hit appearance in the two-game series, dropping his average to .400. AP PHOTO

Logic suggests that if two hitters performed different great deeds in the same season, and no one has been able duplicate either one, then they were feats of equal merit worthy of equal acclaim, and that neither one is going to happen again anytime soon.

Obviously, both DiMaggio's streak and Wiiliams' .406 were prodigious accomplishments that stand as the capstones of their baseball resumes. Only a member of the Hall of Fame's elite could have done either.

There are fluky 25-game hitting streaks. Norm Cash, a career .271 hitter, batted .361 in 1961. But only a player of Brett's caliber could approach .400, just as Pete Rose's 44-game streak in 1978 was the only genuine threat to DiMaggio's record.

In an ideal universe, Williams' and DiMaggio's 1941 feats would be eternally savored and never compared. But this isn't an ideal universe. The MVP voters of 1941 had to decide whether Williams or DiMaggio deserved more credit for what they did and chose DiMaggio, a verdict that history has silently ratified through the decades.

Now that both players are gone, and the debate is purely historic, perhaps the verdict needs review. Williams' .406 should stand above a mere hitting streak much as Hank Aaron's 755 career homers rank him ahead of Mark McGwire for hitting 70 homers in one season.

The hallmark of both DiMaggio's and Williams' efforts was consistency, a defiance of baseball's natural odds for weeks and months at a time. It takes a phenomenal combination of ability and good fortune to avoid going 0 for 4 for 56 consecutive games. DiMaggio's streak ended in luck, when Cleveland third baseman Ken Keltner twice robbed him on line drives.

Had that happened to DiMaggio in Game 18 of the streak, there'd be no record, and DiMaggio would be less of a legend today, even though it wouldn't have diminished his stature as a player at all.

Fans in 1941 had reason to applaud Williams, and they did. But they also had ample reason to believe that hitters in future seasons, including Ted himself, would hit .400 again.

No one, including Williams, ever did. There have been many, many great hitters in the past 60 years, but only one batter actually flirted with .400 deep into September, when George Brett hit .390 in 1980. Only two others, Rod Carew in 1977 and Williams in 1957, had an average as high as .388 for a full season. Tony Gwynn hit .394 in strike-shortened 1994.

BAT MAN: By the time Ted returned to Yankee Stadium on July 1, he had a firm grasp on .400, and Joe DiMaggio's streak was at 42 games

AP PHOTO

DAY-BY-DAY

DATE	GAME	OPP.	RBI	RUNS	AVG.	TOTALS
APR. 15	1-1 (pinch hit single)	Wash.	1	0	1.000	1-1
APR. 16	0-1 (ph)	Wash.			.500	1-2
APR. 17	Rainout vs. Wash.					
APR. 18	1-1 (pinch hit single)	at Phil.			.667	2-3
APR. 19	DNP	at Phil.				
APR. 20	0-1 (pinch hitter)	at Wash.			.500	2-4
APR. 21	0-1 (pinch hitter)	at Wash.			.400	2-5
APR. 22	2-4 (sgl,dbl, 1st start)	at Wash.	2	1	.444	4-9
APR. 23	DNP	at N.Y.				
APR. 24	0-1 (pinch hitter)	at N.Y.			.400	4-10
APR. 25	DNP	Phil.				
APR. 26	DNP	Phil.				
APR. 27	Rainout vs. Phila.					
APR. 28	Day off					
APR. 29	2-3 (HR, double)	at Det.	1	2	.462	6-13
APR. 30	1-5 (single)	at Det.	1		.389	7-18
MAY 1	1-5 (single)	at Det.	1	2	.348	8-23
MAY 2	0-3	at Clev.			.308	8-26
MAY 3	1-3 (single)	at Clev.			.310	9-29
MAY 4	2-5 (2 singles)	at St.L.	2	1	.324	11-34
MAY 5,6	Rainout at St. Louis					
MAY 7	3-4 (2 HR, single)	at Chi.	3	2	.468	14-38
MAY 8	Rained out at Chicago					
MAY 9	Day off					
MAY 10	Rainout vs. N.Y. Yankees					
MAY 11	3-6 (2 singles, double)	N.Y.	1	2	.386	17-44
MAY 12	1-3 (single)	N.Y.		2	.383	18-47
MAY 13	1-4 (HR)	Chi.	1	1	.373	19-51
MAY 14	0-5	Chi.			.336	19-56
MAY 15	1-3 (single)	Clev.		2	.339	20-59
MAY 16	1-4 (single)	Clev.		1	.333	21-63
MAY 17	3-5 (2 doubles, single)	Clev.	1	1	.353	24-68
MAY 18	1-4 (single)	Det.			.347	25-72
MAY 19	1-4 (HR)	Det.	2	1	.342	26-76
MAY 20	1-3 (single)	Det.	1		.341	27-79
MAY 21	4-5 (3 singles, doubles)	St. L.	1		.369	31-84
MAY 22	2-4 (2 singles)	St. L			.375	33-88
MAY 23	1-3 (single)	at N.Y.	3		.374	34-91
MAY 24	2-3 (2 singles)	at N.Y.	3		.383	36-94
MAY 25	4-5 (3 singles, double)	at N.Y.	2	2	.404	40-99
MAY 26	Day off					
MAY 27	1-2 (HR)	Phil.	2	1	.406	41-101
MAY 27	1-4 (single)	Phil.			.400	42-105
MAY 28	3-5 (2 singles, double)	Phil.		1	.409	45-110
MAY 29	3-4 (HR, 2 singles)	Phil.	2	2	.421	48-114
MAY 30	1-2 (double)	N.Y.		2	.422	49-116
MAY 30	2-3 (2 singles)	N.Y.	1	2	.429	51-119
MAY 31	Rainout at Detroit					
JUNE 1	2-4 (double, single)	at Det.	1	2	.431	53-123
JUNE 1	2-5 (HR, single)	at Det.	3	2	.430	55-128
JUNE 2	1-4 (single)	at Det.	1	2	.424	56-132
JUNE 3,4	Rainout at Cleveland					

To hit .400 requires an equal combination of ability and good fortune, and Williams had to maintain it for 154 games, not 56. The math of .400 is more unforgiving than that of a batting streak. One bloop single got DiMaggio off the hook until the next game. An 0-for-4 day meant Williams needed a 4-for-4 day to compensate for taking a collar.

One more baseball argument for giving Williams' 1941 more luster than DiMaggio's: In addition to his 185 hits in 456 at-bats, Ted drew 185 walks. His .551 on-base percentage (not a stat kept at the time) is the best ever.

Williams' .406 even had a superior element of stagecraft. It ought to be more mythic than it is.

As is well known, Ted was hitting .3996 going into the season's final day, a doubleheader against the Athletics. He was offered the chance to sit out as soon as his average reached .400.

Williams, of course, declined, playing until darkness stopped the second game and going 6 for 8 in the process. This was the perfect example of how Williams' unmatched self-confidence and love of the spotlight made him Babe Ruth's equal in dramatics as well as Ty Cobb's peer as a hitter.

If Williams had gone 2 for 8 that day and wound up at .3992, he'd still have been just as great a ballplayer. But his legend also would have been diminished.

Williams got the hits he needed, and his legend got the benchmark it needed. Myths must be salted with facts. Williams' claim as the best hitter who ever lived doesn't rest solely on 1941. But Williams' legend starts with the fact he's the last man to bat .400.

It's a fact that grows in stature with each new season. If .406 isn't as hallowed a baseball number as DiMaggio's 56, it should be.

ACCOUNT OF THE 1941 SEASON

DATE	GAME	OPP.	RBI	RUNS	AVG.	TOTALS
JUNE 5	3-4 (HR, 2 singles)	at Clev.	3	4	.434	59-136
JUNE 6	2-4 (HR, double)	at Chi.	2	2	.436	61-140
JUNE 7	1-4 (single)	at Chi.		1	.431	62-144
JUNE 8	0-2	at Chi.	1		.425	62-146
JUNE 8	0-3	at Chi.	1		.416	62-149
JUNE 9	Exhibition at Indianapolis					
JUNE 10,11	Rainout at St. Louis					
JUNE 12	1-5 (single)	at St.L.			.409	63-154
JUNE 12	1-2 (HR)	at St.L.	2	1	.410	64-156
JUNE 13	Day off					
JUNE 14	3-5 (double, 2 singles)	Chi.			.416	67-161
JUNE 15	2-3 (single, HR)	Chi.	1	2	.421	69-164
JUNE 15	2-3 (2 singles)	Chi.	1	2	.425	71-167
JUNE 16	Day off					
JUNE 17	1-4 (HR)	Det.	2	1	.421	72-171
JUNE 17	1-1 (double)	Det.		2	.424	73-172
JUNE 18	0-3	Det.			.417	73-175
JUNE 19	1-3 (single)	Det.	2		.416	74-178
JUNE 20	2-3 (single, double)	St.L.	2	1	.420	76-181
JUNE 21	0-2	St.L.		1	.415	76-183
JUNE 22	1-3 (single)	St.L.	2	1	.414	77-186
JUNE 22	0-3	St.L			.407	77-189
JUNE 23	Day off					
JUNE 24	0-2	Clev.		2	.403	77-191
JUNE 25	2-3 (HR, single)	Clev.	2	2	.407	79-194
JUNE 26	3-5 (3 singles)	Clev.	1	2	.412	82-199
JUNE 27	1-3 (single)	at Wash.			.411	83-202
JUNE 28	1-3 (single)	at Wash.			.410	84-205
JUNE 29	2-4 (HR, single)	at Phil.	2	2	.410	86-209
JUNE 29	0-4	at Phil.	1		.404	86-213
JUNE 30	Day off					
JULY 1	1-4 (single)	at N.Y.			.401	87-217
JULY 1	1-2 (single)	at N.Y.	1		.402	88-219
JULY 2	1-3 (single)	at N.Y.	1		.401	89-222
JULY 3	2-4 (HR, single)	at Phil.	2	2	.403	91-226
JULY 4	Rainout at Phila.					
JULY 5	1-3 (double)	Wash.	1	1	.402	92-229
JULY 6	1-4 (single)	Wash.	1		.399	93-233
JULY 6	3-4 (2 doubles, single)	Wash.	2	2	.405	96-237
JULY 7,8,9	All-Star break					
JULY 10	Rainout at Detroit					
JULY 11	0-4	at Det.			.398	96-241
JULY 12	0-1	at Det.	2		.397	96-242
JULY 12	DNP	at Det.				
JULY 13	DNP	at Clev.				
JULY 14	DNP (injured ankle)	at Clev.				
JULY 15	DNP					
JULY 16	0-1 (sacrifice fly)	at Chi.	1		.395	96-243
JULY 17	DNP	at Chi.				
JULY 18	DNP	at Chi.				
JULY 19	0-1	at St.L.			.393	96-244
JULY 19	0-0 (walk)	at St.L.				

DATE	GAME	OPP.	RBI	RUNS	AVG.	TOTALS
JULY 20	1-1 (ph HR)	at St.L.	3	1	.396	97-245
JULY 20	DNP a	t St.L.				
JULY 21	Day off					
JULY 22	1-2 (HR)	Chi.	1	1	.397	98-247
JULY 23	2-5 (double, single)	Chi.		1	.397	100-252
JULY 24	2-5 (2 singles)	Chi.		1	.397	102-257
JULY 25	2-3 (HR, single)	Clev.	2	3	.400	104-260
JULY 26	3-4 (3 singles)	Clev.		1	.405	107-264
JULY 27	2-3 (single, double)	Clev.			.408	109-267
JULY 28	Day off					
JULY 29	1-3 (HR)	St. L.	2	1	.407	110-270
JULY 30	Rainout vs. St. Louis					
JULY 31	2-3 (grand slam, single)	St. L.	4	2	.410	112-273
JULY 31	1-3 (double)	St. L.			.409	113-276
AUG. 1	Day off (Ted catches					
	374-pound tuna					
AUG. 2	2-3 (double, single)	Det.		1	.412	115-279
AUG. 3	1-4 (single)	Det.			.410	116-283
AUG. 4	0-2	Phil.			.407	116-285
AUG. 5	2-4 (double, single)	Phil.	2	1	.408	118-289
AUG. 6	1-3 (single)	N.Y.			.408	119-292
AUG. 6	0-3	N.Y.			.403	119-295
AUG. 7	3-4 (HR, 2 singles)	N.Y.	2	3	.408	122-299
AUG. 8	1-3 (single)	Wash.		2	.407	123-302
AUG. 9	1-3 (single)	Wash.		1	.407	124-305
AUG. 10	3-4 (2 singles, triple)	Wash.			.411	127-309
AUG. 10	1-3 (single)	Wash.			.410	128-312
AUG. 11	1-1 (single)	at N.Y.	1	1	.412	129-313
AUG. 12	1-3 (single)	at N.Y.			.411	130-316
AUG. 13	1-1 (double)	at Phil.	1		.413	131-317
AUG. 14	1-5 (HR)	at Phil.	3	2	.410	132-322
AUG. 14	1-4 (single)	at Phil.		1	.408	133-326
AUG. 15	0-2	at Wash.			.405	133-328
AUG. 16	3-5 (double, 2 singles)	at Wash.	1	2	.408	136-333
AUG. 17	0-3	at Wash.			.405	136-336
AUG. 18	Rainout at St. Louis					
AUG. 19	1-3 (HR)	at St.L.	1	1	.404	137-339
AUG. 19	4-5 (2 HR, 2 singles)	at St.L.	3	2	.410	141-344
AUG. 20	2-4 (HR, single)	at St.L.	2	3	.411	143-348
AUG. 20	1-2 (HR)	at St.L.	2	1	.411	144-350
AUG. 21	2-3 (2 singles)	at Chi.		2	.414	146-353
AUG. 22	0-2	at Chi.	1		.411	146-355
AUG. 23	1-4 (single)	at Chi.			.409	147-359
AUG. 24	1-4 (single)	at Clev.		1	.408	148-363
AUG. 24	0-3	at Clev.			.404	148-366
AUG. 25	0-2	at Clev.		1	.402	148-368
AUG. 26	1-1 (single)	at Clev.			.404	149-369
AUG. 27	2-4 (2 singles)	at Det.	1		.405	151-373
AUG. 28	2-3 (HR, triple)	at Det.	1	2	.407	153-376
AUG. 29	Day off					
AUG. 30	2-3 (HR, single)	Phil.	2	3	.409	155-379
AUG. 31	1-3 (HR)	Phil.	3	1	.408	156-382

DATE	GAME	OPP.	RBI	RUNS	AVG.	TOTALS
AUG. 31	0-1	Phil.			.407	156-383
SEPT. 1	2-3 (2 HR)	Wash.	4	2	.409	158-386
SEPT. 1	1-2 (HR)	Wash.	1	3	.410	159-388
SEPT. 2	Day off					
SEPT. 3	1-3 (single)	N.Y.			.409	160-391
SEPT. 4	1-1 (single)	N.Y.		1	.411	161-392
SEPT. 5	Day off					
SEPT. 6	1-4 (single)	at N.Y.	1	1	.409	162-396
SEPT. 7	3-4 (2 doubles, single)	at N.Y.	1	1	.413	165-400
SEPT. 8	Day off					
SEPT. 9	1-3 (single)	Det.			.412	166-403
SEPT. 10	2-4 (double, single)	Det.	3	1	.413	168-407
SEPT. 11	Day off					
SEPT. 12	0-3	St.L.		1	.410	168-410
SEPT. 13	0-1	St.L.			.409	168-411
SEPT. 14	2-3 (double, single)	Chi.	1	1	.411	170-414
SEPT. 14	1-4 (triple)	Chi.	1	1	.409	171-418
SEPT. 15	1-3 (HR)	Chi.	3	1	.409	172-421
SEPT. 16	Day off					
SEPT. 17	1-3 (double)	Clev.			.408	173-424
SEPT. 18	0-3	Clev.			.405	173-427
SEPT. 19	Day off					
SEPT. 20	2-4 (singles)	N.Y.			.406	175-431
SEPT. 21	1-3 (HR)	N.Y.	2	1	.406	176-434
SEPT. 22	Day off					
SEPT. 23	1-3 (double)	at Wash.		1	.405	177-437
SEPT. 24	0-3	at Wash.		1	.401	178-440
SEPT. 24	1-4 (single)	at Wash.		1	.401	178-444
SEPT. 25,26	Days off					
SEPT. 27	1-4 (double)	at Phil.		1	.400	179-448
SEPT. 28	4-5 (HR, 3 singles)	at Phil.	2	2	.404	183-453
SEPT. 28	2-3 (double, single)	at Phil.			.406	185-456

SEASON TOTALS

AB— 456; R— 135; H— 185; 2B— 33; 3B— 3;
HR— 37; RBI— 120; SP%— .735; AVG.— .406.

NOTE— His longest hitless streak of the season was 0-7 over 4 games. He is the youngest player ever to hit .400 in a season turning 23 during the season. Others who hit .400 at a young age were:

Ty Cobb ....at 24, hit .420 in 1911.
Joe Jackson ....at 24, hit .408 in 1911.
Nap Lajoie ....at 26, hit .422 in 1901.
Rogers Hornsby ....at 26, hit .401 in 1922.
George Sisler ....at 27, hit .407 in 1920.
Harry Heilmann ....at 29, hit .403 in 1923.
Bill Terry ....at 31, hit .401 in 1930.

THE LAST HURRAH

WILLIAMS BOWED OUT IN SPECTACULAR STYLE

Karen Guregian

Ray Bourque got it right when he retired last year after reaching the pinnacle of his 22-year NHL career by winning his only championship with the Colorado Avalanche. Clenching the Stanley Cup and raising it above his head was his final act as a hockey player, the exclamation point on his storied career. It really doesn't get better than that, at least not for most athletes — superstars or otherwise. Ted Williams, however, came close. He didn't win a World Series with his final swing, but he did slug a home run in his last plate appearance. He went out with the ultimate hit, and he did it before a home crowd at Fenway Park on Wednesday, Sept. 28, 1960.

The greatest hitter who ever lived retired with one last stroll around the bases, with one last homer, No. 521 in the record books.

The moment was so grand, so spectacular, noted author John Updike memorialized the event by penning the now famous work, "Hub Fans Bid Kid Adieu," in *The New Yorker* magazine. Updike was in the stands that afternoon as the Sox took on the Baltimore Orioles.

He was seated behind third base, scripting the events as they took place. It was Updike who called Fenway a "lyric little bandbox of a ballpark" in the first sentence of his classic piece.

This was the Sox' last home game of the season, and, in Updike's prose, "the last time in all eternity that their regular left fielder, known to the headlines as TED, KID, SPLINTER, THUMPER, TW, and, most cloyingly, MISTER WONDERFUL, would play in Boston."

Williams was 42. He had threatened retirement before, only to return, but most believed it was real this time.

He didn't have the best year in 1959, hitting just .254 with 10 homers. Even though club owner Tom Yawkey had asked him to hang it up, No. 9 came back one more season to show he wasn't exactly washed up. He even took a voluntary pay cut from $125,000 to $95,000 — and proceeded to hit a robust .316 with 29 home runs.

Before that final Fenway game, the Kid gave away his gloves and bats, and there was a pregame ceremony paying homage to the great one. Then Sox broadcaster Curt Gowdy emceed the proceedings. In his closing remarks, he proclaimed of Wliams: "I don't think we'll ever see another like him."

That day, Teddy Ballgame was batting third in the order. In his first at-bat in the bottom of first against Steve Barber, he walked on four pitches. In the third, he flied out to deep center. In the fifth, most thought he had hit one out as he crushed one to deep right. However, it was caught at the 380-foot sign, against the bullpen fence, by Al Pilarcik.

"Damn," Williams said when he returned

to the bench at the end of the inning, as recounted from an excerpt in Ed Linn's book, *Hitter: The Life and Turmoils of Ted Williams.* "I hit the living hell out of that one, I really stung it. If that one didn't go out, nothing is going out today."

With the Sox trailing 4-2, he batted one final time in the eighth inning against Orioles reliever Jack Fisher. He was the second batter up in the inning.

When leadoff hitter Willie Tasby emerged from the dugout, with Williams not far behind, the cheering started.

Then, when the Splendid Splinter finally got to the plate, it was almost surreal. Sensing it would be the legend's last at-bat, the Fenway faithful — all 10,454 of them — rose and gave him a standing ovation like no other. It lasted nearly two minutes.

Wrote Updike: "I had never before heard pure applause in the ballpark. No calling, no whistling, just an ocean of handclaps, minute after minute, burst after burst, crowding and running together in continuous succession like the pushes of surf at the edge of sand. It was a somber and considered tumult. There was not a boo in it. It seemed to renew itself out of a shifting set of memories as the Kid, the Marine, the veteran of feuds and failures and injuries, the friend of the children, and the enduring old pro evolved down the bright tunnel of 22 summers toward this moment."

The first pitch was low for ball one. Williams then swung mightily and missed the second. It was clear to everyone in the park what he had in mind. Finally, on the third pitch, a fastball Fisher threw much higher than intended, Williams connected.

Once it left the bat, there was no doubt.

Penned Updike: "The ball climbed on a diagonal line into the vast volume of air over center field ... it struck in the crotch where the bullpen met the wall, bounced chunkily and vanished."

Williams strode around the bases in his typical fashion — galloping in a brisk trot, with his head down.

The crowd exploded, filling the air with

cheers. Soon, they chanted, "We want Ted! We want Ted! We want Ted!"

Only, Williams didn't acknowledge their praise. He didn't tip his cap, and he didn't come out for a curtain call, even though he was practically begged to do so.

"Gods do not answer letters," Updike wrote.

At the end of the inning, Sox manager Mike Higgins sent Williams out to left field, then immediately replaced him with Carrol Hardy.

Williams jogged in, once again, with his head down while people stood and passionately applauded.

Still, no sign of appreciation from Ted. The only thing Williams did after heading back into the dugout was send his home run bat up to Mr. Yawkey. Years later, Williams, who didn't exactly have the best rapport with the fans, not to mention the media, was asked why he didn't recognize the crowd, why he chose to leave in such a bittersweet fashion.

In Linn's book, *Hitter*, Ted gave his version.

"Let me tell you something. When I hit the ball, I was obviously hoping it would go, and there it went," Williams said. "Now I have great elation. In my mind as I'm rounding first base, I say, 'God' ... I thought about my hat, and I thought about it. I hit second base, and I said, 'No, I'll never tip my hat.' And I came into home plate more than ever convinced that I wouldn't. It was that type of feeling. Then when I ran into the dugout, and they're all coming to me and asking me to come on out, come on out, and I didn't do it. That was my feeling going round the bases. Somewhere around hitting second base and going to third, that's where I said no."

There were still more games to play on the schedule, but Williams had decided to end it with that electrifying Fenway homer. He opted not to accompany the team to New York for the final series of the season. He called it quits right then and there.

That apparently had been the plan. Although there were reports to dispute this scenario, the story spun by the Sox was that Williams wasn't going to the Big Apple unless the pennant race was still alive.

THE FINAL SWING: After addressing the Fenway faithful (top left) before his final game on Sept. 28, 1960, Ted Williams smacked a home run in his last at-bat. Despite cries from the crowd, he refused to tip his cap. The Last Hurrah Williams bowed out in spectacular style.

PHOTO COURTESY OF THE BREARLEY COLLECTION

So he left with one last swing for the books, one last highlight for his incredible legacy.

"I was gunning for the big one," Williams was quoted as saying after the game, which the Sox eventually won, 5-4. "I let everything I had go. I really wanted that one."

Ultimately, he would start and finish his final season on the same note. In his first at-bat of that memorable '60 season, Williams blasted one of the longest homers he hit in his career. It was a 500-foot moon shot off Camilo Pascual.

Then, in his last, he hit perhaps his most dramatic.

Wrote Updike: "The ball seemed less an object in flight than the tip of a towering, montionless construct, like the Eiffel Tower or the Tappan Zee Bridge. It was in the books while it was still in the sky."

It was one of those rare sendoffs. One befitting of a legend.

THE LIFE & TIMES

A CHRONOLOGICAL LOOK AT THE LIFE OF BASEBALL'S GREATEST HITTER

Karen Guregian

1918

AUG. 30– Born in San Diego to Sam Williams and May Venzer.

1936

JUNE 26– 17-year-old Williams signed by San Diego Padres of Pacific Coast League.

JULY– Eddie Collins, Red Sox general manager, first notices Williams during scouting trip in Portland, Ore.

1937

FEBRUARY– Williams graduates from Hoover High School in San Diego.

DECEMBER 1– Collins purchases Williams' contract from Padres for $25,000 & $25,000 worth of ballplayers.

1938

MARCH 21– In first Red Sox spring training, Williams optioned to Minneapolis Millers of American Association.

SEPTEMBER 11– Williams finishes season at Minneapolis with .366 batting average, 43 home runs, 142 RBIs.

1939

APRIL 20– Williams goes 1 for 4 (double) at Yankee Stadium in first major-league game. Hit comes off of Red Ruffing.

APRIL 23– At Fenway Park, hits first major-league home run, off A's Luther Thomas.

SEPTEMBER– Williams finishes rookie season hitting .327, 31 home runs and league-high 145 RBIs.

1941

MAY 15– Williams begins 23-game hitting streak, the same day Joe DiMaggio begins his record 56-game hitting streak.

JUNE 8– Williams ends hitting streak, during which he hit .488.

JULY 8– Williams' ninth-inning home run wins All-Star Game.

JULY 23– In attempt to capitalize on Williams' tendency to pull ball down right field line, White Sox manager Jimmy Dykes is first manager to use infield shift, in which third baseman plays at shortstop and shortstop and second baseman play between first and second.

SEPT. 27– On next-to-last day of season, Williams' average "dips" to .3996.

SEPT. 28– In doubleheader, Williams goes 6 for 8 to lift average to .406. No one has hit .400 since.

1942

MAY 22– Enlists in U.S. Naval Air Corps.

OCT. 1– Williams wins Triple Crown: .356, 36 home runs, 137 RBIs.

DEC. 8– Williams inducted into Navy.

1944

MAY 4– Marries Doris Soule of Princeton, Minn.

1946

JAN. 2– Returns from service.

MARCH 3– Upon return from the service, Williams homers and knocks in seven runs in his first exhibition game.

JUNE 9– Hits home run that lands 33 rows up in right-field bleachers at Fenway Park, knocking hole through straw hat of spectator Joe Boucher.

JULY 9– Collects four hits, two for home runs, and five RBIs in All-Star Game at Fenway Park.

JULY 21– Hits for cycle.

SEPT. 13– In Cleveland, hits his only inside-the-park home run, which is also is his first home run to left field.

SEPT. 3– On eve of World Series between Red Sox and Cardinals, trade rumor printed that Red Sox were going to trade Williams to Yankees (for DiMaggio), Detroit or Cleveland.

OCT. 14– Hits .200, Red Sox lose World Series to Cardinals in seven games.

WINTER– Wins American League MVP Award: .342, 38 home runs, 123 RBIs.

1947

OCTOBER 1– Wins second Triple Crown: .343, 32 home runs, 114 RBIs.

NOVEMBER– Loses AL MVP award by one vote to DiMaggio.

1948

JAN. 28– Daughter born in Boston while Williams fishing in Florida. He arrives in Boston five days later.

1949

SEPTEMBER, 1949– Barely loses third Triple Crown with .34275 batting average, trailing Detroit Tiger George Kell's .34291.

OCT. 1– Wins second American League MVP award: .343, 43 home runs, career-high 159 RBIs.

1950

JULY 14– Fractures left elbow at All-Star Game by running into Comiskey Park scoreboard.

1952

APRIL 30– In final game before leaving for Korean War, hits game-winning home run.

MAY 3– At age 33, begins active duty with Marines for Korean War.

1953

FEB. 16– Hit by enemy fire, Williams lands plane safely.

JULY 29– Resumes working out with Red Sox after returning from Korean War.

1954

MARCH 1– Breaks collarbone on first day of spring training.

MAY 7– Makes first start of season at Detroit doubleheader: two home runs, double, two singles, seven RBIs.

SEPT. 27– Announces retirement from baseball.

1955

MAY 9– Williams and Soule divorced.

MAY 24– Hits home run in first game back from "retirement."

1956

JULY 17– Hits 400th home run.

1957

JUNE 13– First American Leaguer to hit three home runs in a game twice in one season.

SEPT. 23– Ties record by hitting home runs in four consecutive at-bats.

1958

SEPT. 21– Throws bat into Fenway Park stands, hits Gladys Hefferman.

SEPT. 28– Wins second consecutive AL batting title (.328); sixth and final batting title of his career.

1960

JUNE 17– Hits 500th home run, against Cleveland

SEPT. 28– At Fenway Park in final at-bat of career, homers off Orioles' Jack Fischer.

1962

1962– Marries Lee Howard.

1964

1964– Divorces Howard.

1966

1966– Elected to Baseball Hall of Fame.

1968

1968– Marries Delores Wettach.

AUG. 27— Son John Henry Williams born.

1969

JANUARY– Begins three-year stint as manager of Washington Senators.

1973

1973– Divorces Wettach.

1978

1978– Named Red Sox consultant, organizational hitting instructor

1991

MAY 12– Ted Williams Day at Fenway Park: Tips his hat.

1995

NOV. 1– Formally inducted into Red Sox Hall of Fame.

1999

JULY 13– Makes final public appearance at All-Star Game at Fenway Park.

2000

NOV 7– Suffering from congestive heart failure, Williams has pacemaker inplanted.

2001

JAN 16– Is in operating room for nine hours during open-heart surgery at Cornell Medical Center in New York.

2002

JULY 5– Dies at age of 83 in Crystal River, Fla.

SOX 'MATES LOVED TED

Mike Shalin

Fans, by their very nature, want to be impressed by their idols. Teammates, on the other hand, usually don't care. Unless, of course, they're the former teammates of Ted Williams. For those lucky enough to have played with Williams, they remember the Hall of Famer as a larger-than-life figure who was a great teammate. Williams' longtime pal, Johnny Pesky, once said: "When you talk about Ted, you're talking about a guy walking on water . . . We all felt that way about him. He was so good to all of us."

Friday night at Fenway, Pesky talked about his last meeting with Williams. "The last time I saw him was this past spring training. I was down in Florida, at his museum. I was sitting next to Enos Slaughter, and they brought Ted out to see everyone. It was a sad moment, 'cause you knew the guy was sick. Enos, he just started crying. But Ted recognized us.

"I got my face to about six inches from his and I said, 'Hi, Ted,' and he said, 'Hey, Johnny, how are you?' And he showed me that smile of his. I figured that's the last time I'd probably see him. But you know how it goes. I got home, and I started to think he'd pull through. He always seemed to fight back, so I'm thinking, yeah, he'll beat this."

Bobby Doerr, who was Williams' teammate for 10 seasons, summed up the feelings of all those who played with the Splendid Splinter. "Ted was a great team player," he said. "He wanted to win. He patted everyone on the back . . . He was a loyal friend. He was ahead of his time in baseball in many ways . . . I think he was the best hitter that baseball has had," Doerr added. "He was the first hitter to go to a lighter bat for quickness. He was the first one to come up with a combination of olive oil and resin to get a better grip on the bat, and then was the first to use pine tar."

Dom DiMaggio, who played alongside Ted Williams for 11 years as the Red Sox center fielder, agreed with Doerr. "Nobody hit a baseball like Ted," DiMaggio once said. "He had that big swing. He'd swing up, over and around the ball."

DiMaggio liked to tell a story in response to those who claimed Williams couldn't hit to left field and that he'd pull the ball even when teams overshifted.

"He could have gone to left anytime he wanted," DiMaggio said. "I like to tell the story about when we were playing in Philadelphia one day and we were facing Jack Wilson, who used to pitch for us.

"We'd scored a lot of runs, but Connie Mack left Jack in there to save his pitching staff. It was late in the game and Ted came to the plate. There'd been this guy in the left-field stands who'd been heckling Ted all day. When Ted had two strikes on him, he kept hitting foul balls to left. He was hitting the ball close to the guy. After hitting 15-16 balls

at the guy, he took a lackadaisical swing and hit the ball off the left center-field wall for a double. He could hit the ball anywhere he wanted."

DiMaggio also raved about Williams' focus on the team.

"He loved his teammates," DiMaggio recalled. "He'd do anything he could to help anyone out. He went his own way, but we respected that. We knew that he was a great teammate."

One teammate whose appreciation of Williams grew during the years was former Sox shortstop and ex-Boston College baseball coach Eddie Pellagrini.

"I always liked the guy," Pellagrini once said. "He was always doing things for people. If he said something bad to someone, he'd always come back later and say he was sorry. For all his loudness, he was like a little boy. I loved the guy.

"I'm always telling people about the year Williams and I hit 48 homers — I hit two," Pellagrini said. "I liked him very much.

"I played for Rogers Hornsby and we were sitting around the dugout talking about hitting. He said he had a better average and all that, but I said Ted was a better hitter. I don't think [Hornsby] liked me after that."

Pellagrini remembers a compassionate Williams.

"He had feelings for everybody in Boston," Pellagrini said. "Even when he was acting up, he would always feel sorry about it afterward.

"He was the greatest hitter I ever saw, one of the most colorful people, a dynamic personality, a handsome guy and a hell of a baseball player."

Mel Parnell also praised his former teammate.

"He's pretty much a super-type person, a perfect individual," Parnell said. "He's a self-made man, and everything he accomplished he did to perfection and did it on his own.

"Ted's sort of different than the rest of us. It seemed like the guy was such a hard worker . . . He's a man I greatly respected."

Pesky summed up the feelings of Ted's teammates as tears welled up in his eyes at Fenway Friday night. "I knew this day was coming. I knew it was coming, but now that it's here, I'm not prepared for it. I'm having a hard time believing Ted's gone, you know?"

Gone, but never to be forgotten by those privileged enough to call him a teammate.

Steve Buckley, Jack O'Leary and *Herald* Wire Services contributed to this report.

Ted Williams Career Statistics

Born August 30, 1918 in San Diego. Batted left. Threw right.
No. 9 was formally retired May 29, 1984

REGULAR SEASON

Category figures below in bold denote league-leading total

	AVG	G	AB	R	H	2B	3B	HR	TB	RBI	BB	SO	SB
1936 San Diego	. 71	4	107	18	9	8		0	41	11	—	—	
1937 San Diego	. 91	138	454	66	13	4		3	9	98	—	—	1
1938 Minneapolis	.366	148	528	**130**	193	30	9	43	**370**	14	**114**	75	6
1939 Boston	.3 7	149	565	131	185	44	11	31	**344**	145	107	64	
1940 Boston	.344	144	561	**134**	193	43	14	3	333	113	96	54	4
1941 Boston	.406	143	456	**135**	185	33	3	**37**	335	120	**145**	27	
1942 Boston	.356	150	5	**141**	186	34	5	**36**	**338**	**137**	**145**	51	3
1943-44-45				In military service									
1946 Boston	.34	150	514	14	176	37	8	38	**343**	1 3	**156**	44	0
1947 Boston	**.343**	156	5 8	1 5	181	40	9	3	**335**	114	16	47	0
1948 Boston	.369	137	509	1 4	188	**44**	3	5	313	1 7	1 6	41	4
1949 Boston	.343	155	566	**150**	194	**39**	3	**43**	**368**	**159**	16	48	1
1950 Boston-a	.317	89	334	8	106	4	1	8	16	97	8	21	3
1951 Boston	.318	148	531	109	169	8	4	30	**95**	1 6	**144**	45	1
1952 Boston-b	.400	6	10		4	0	1	1	9	3			0
1953 Boston-b	.407	37	91	17	37	6	0	13	8	34	19	10	0
1954 Boston	.345	117	386	93	133	3	1	9	45	89	**136**	3	0
1955 Boston	.356	98	320	77	114	1	3	8	5	83	91	4	
1956 Boston	.345	136	400	71	138	8		4	4	8	10	39	0
1957 Boston	**.388**	13	4 0	96	163	8	1	38	307	87	119	43	0
1958 Boston	.3 8	1 9	411	81	135	3		6	40	85	98	49	1
1959 Boston	. 54	103	7	3	69	15	0	10	114	43	5	7	0
1960 Boston	.316	113	310	56	98	15	0	9	200	7	75	41	1
M.L. Totals	**.344**	9	7706	1798	654	5 5	71	5 1	4884	1839	019	709	4

a — Suffered fractured left elbow when he crashed into the left field wall making catch in first inning of All-Star Game at Chicago, July 11, 1950. Despite the injury, he stayed in the game until the 9th inning. Played in only 19 more games the rest of the season.
b — In military service most of the season.

WORLD SERIES RECORD

	AVG	G	AB	R	H	2B	3B	HR	RBI	BB	SO	E
1946 vs. St. Louis	.200	7	5		5	0	0	0	1	5	5	0

TED BY THE NUMBERS

Ted Williams stands on Red Sox' all-time list

HOME RUNS
Williams..............5 1
Yastrzemski 45
Rice...............................38
Evans 379
Doerr.............................. 3

GAMES
Yastrzemski................3,308
Evans..........................2,505
Williams.......................2, 9
Rice............................2,089
Doerr..........................1,865

HITS
Yastrzemski 3,419
Williams.....................2,654
Rice.............................2,45
Evans 2,373
Boggs.........................2,098

EXTRA-BASE HITS
Yastrzemski...............1,157
Williams.....................1,117
Evans 9 5
Rice...............................834
Doerr.............................693

ON BASE PCT.
Williams........................ .483
Foxx 4 9
Boggs 4 8
Speaker 414
Runnels......................... .408

RUNS BATTED IN
Yastrzemski................1,844
Ted Williams..............1,839
Rice............................1,451
Evans..........................1,346
Doerr..........................1, 47

AT BATS
Yastrzemski 11,988
Evans............................8,7 6
Rice.............................8, 5
Williams.....................7,706
Doerr..........................7,093

DOUBLES
Yastrzemski..................646
Williams 5 5
Evans............................474
Boggs 4
Doerr.............................381

SLUGGING PCT.
Williams 634
Foxx .... .605
Lynn.............................. .520
Rice .... .50
V. Stephens .... .49

FENWAY HOME RUNS**
Williams 48
Yastrzemski 37
Rice...............................208
Evans............................199
Doerr.............................145

BATTING AVG.*
Ted Williams...................344
Boggs.............................338
Speaker .... .337
Foxx 320
Runnels 320

RUNS
Yastrzemski 1,816
Williams 1,798
Evans 1,435
Rice 1, 49
Doerr............................1,094

TOTAL BASES
Yastrzemski..................5,539
Williams......................4,884
Rice.............................4,129
Evans 4,1 8
Doerr 3, 70

WALKS
Williams......................2,019
Yastrzemski....................1,845
Evans...........................1,337
Boggs 1,004
Hooper 8 6

*Minimum 1,500 at-bats
**Red Sox only

Career Highlights

- Named to Hall of Fame in Cooperstown, 1966.
- Named Major League Player of the Decade for 1950s.
- American League Most Valuable Player, 1946 and 1949.
- Named to starting outfield of Greatest Living Team.
- Won AL Triple Crown, 1942 and 1947.
- Led AL in Batting, 1941-4 -47-48-57-58.
- Led AL in Home Runs, 1941-4 -47-49.
- Led AL in Walks, 1941-4 -46-47-48-49-51-54.
- Led AL in Total Bases, 1939-4 -46-47-51.
- Led AL in Slugging Pct., 1941-4 -46-47-48-49-51-54-57.
- Holds ML record for most successive times reaching base safely, 16, in Sept., 1957 (2 singles, 4 HR, 9 BB, 1 HBP).
- Oldest ML player to win a batting title when he hit .388 in 1957 at age 39 and then won again in 1958 at 40.
- Holds ML record for most consecutive years leading league in walks, 6.
- Voted Greatest Red Sox Player of all time by fans, 1969 and 1982.
- Hit for the cycle, July 21, 1946.
- Hit three home runs in one game three times (7/14/46, 5/8/57, 6/13/57).
- Holds major-league rookie records for most RBIs, 145, and walks, 107.
- Hit 17 grand slams (Red Sox record).
- Tied for A.L.record with Babe Ruth, most years 20 or more HR, 16.
- *Sporting News* No. 1 Major League Player, 1941-4 -47-49-57.
- Managed Washington-Texas, 1969-7 .
- Named Red Sox consultant, organizational hitting instructor, 1978.
- Member of Hall of Fame's Committee on Veterans, 1986-2002.

Ted's Home Run Milestones

NO. 1 April 23, 1939 vs. Philadelphia at Fenway off A's Bud Thomas.

NO. 100 May 21, 1942 in Cleveland off Indians' Joe Krakauskas.

NO. 200 April 9, 1948 at Philadelphia off A's Bill McCahan.

NO. 300 May 15, 1951 vs. Chicago at Fenway off White Sox' Howie Judson.

NO. 400 July 17, 1956 vs. Kansas City at Fenway (2nd game) off A's Tom Gorman.

NO. 500 June 17, 1960 at Cleveland off Indians' Wynn Hawkins.

NO. 521 September 8, 1960 vs. Baltimore at Fenway off Orioles' Jack Fisher in final career at-bat.

Ted Williams vs. Opponents

VS. AMERICAN LEAGUE

	AB	H	HR	RBI	AVG
Vs. Balt.	310	10	0	66	.3 9
Vs. Chi.	1,1 5	364	65	44	.3 4
Vs. Clev.	1,1 7	361	79	65	.320
Vs. Det.	1,167	386	88	83	.331
Vs. KC A's	3 7	120	5	74	.367
Vs. N.Y.	1,035	357	¯6	9	.345
Vs. Phil. A's	768	81	66	4	.366
Vs. St.L.	754	96	60	3	.393
Vs. Was.	1,093	387	56	31	.354

OVER HALF-SEASONS

	AB	H	HR	RBI	AVG
First Half	3,743	1, 70	51	937	.339
Second Half	3,963	1,384	70	90	.349

AS A PINCH-HITTER

AB	H	HR	RBI	AVG
111	33	7	34	. 97

MONTH-BY-MONTH

	AB	H	HR	RBI	AVG
April	468	156	31	108	.333
May	1, 97	436	95	341	.336
June	1,500	50	97	378	.335
July	1,541	545	108	345	.354
August	1,597	544	101	367	.341
September	1, 83	461	88	93	.359
October	0	10	1	7	.500

LONGEST HITTING STREAK

3 games in 1941, the year he hit .406.

Ted Williams Home & Away

	AB	H	HR	RBI	AVG		AB	H	HR	RBI	AVG
At Fenway	3,887	1,403	48	965	.361	Away	3,819	1, 51	73	874	.3 8

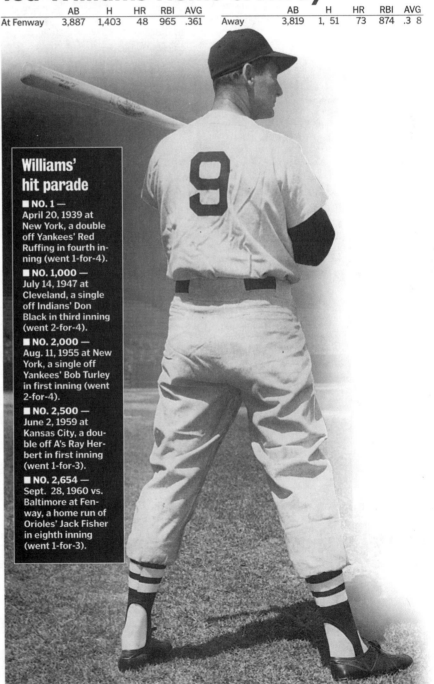

Williams' hit parade

■ NO. 1 — April 20, 1939 at New York, a double off Yankees' Red Ruffing in fourth inning (went 1-for-4).

■ NO. 1,000 — July 14, 1947 at Cleveland, a single off Indians' Don Black in third inning (went 2-for-4).

■ NO. 2,000 — Aug. 11, 1955 at New York, a single off Yankees' Bob Turley in first inning (went 2-for-4).

■ NO. 2,500 — June 2, 1959 at Kansas City, a double off A's Ray Herbert in first inning (went 1-for-3).

■ NO. 2,654 — Sept. 28, 1960 vs. Baltimore at Fenway, a home run of Orioles' Jack Fisher in eighth inning (went 1-for-3).

"I've never seen a better hitter: not just hit, but power. He was feared. He was a devastating hitter: He had such a great eye. I could see that from center field."

JOE DIMAGGIO ON TED WILLIAMS

TWO GOOD TO BE TRUE

WILLIAMS, DIMAGGIO BATTLED FOR SUPREMACY DURING BASEBALL'S GOLDEN AGE

Dave Cataneo

SHOP TALK: Ted Williams and Joe Dimaggio talk baseball before a game at Fenway Park on August 18, 1942, a year after their legendary 1941 season. *HERALD FILE PHOTO*

Joe DiMaggio had just posed for photographs with Ted Williams, and after the hand clasping and shoulder slapping and Vivitar flashes were over, the Red Sox legend swept out of the room one way and the Yankee legend walked out another.

"We've never had a chance to be close," said DiMaggio in an empty corridor. The regal Yankee legend was at the Wang Center on that early evening in the fall of '88, on hand for a Jimmy Fund tribute to Williams. "We've never gone out to dinner together, or gone fishing, or really been alone. We really have only seen each other at functions. In that sense, there really hasn't been a relationship between the two of us."

In the hearts and minds of generations of baseball fans, of course, Ted Williams and Joe DiMaggio couldn't have been closer. If they had never played against each other, or never shared a banquet table together, hardball historians would still feel compelled to compare them. Babe Ruth never had so much as a cup of coffee with Hank Aaron.

But fate plopped DiMaggio and Williams into the same era, so Joe vs. Ted was something a whole generation could argue, over its Ballantine and Gansett.

Joe D. vs. Ted? Both are gone, but the discussion retains its freshness.

"It was either Ted or it was me," said DiMaggio. "That's baseball and that's the way it will be 1,000 years from now. That kind of thing will be part of the game.

"In a sense, it was flattering. What people were saying was that, at the time, we were the two best."

Who wouldn't compare? One was in New York, one was in Boston. One batted righty at Yankee Stadium, the other lefty at Fenway Park. One was tweed jacket dignified, the other neon loud. One was an outstanding hitter, brilliant fielder, and skillful base runner. The other was maybe the greatest hitter who ever lived.

So even if they never went fishing together, they found their names often in the same sentence.

"What we've had is an admiration for one another, more than anything else," said DiMaggio.

In a baseball sense, they were an item.

"Absolutely, he was the best hitter I ever saw," said DiMaggio. "I've never seen a better hitter. Not just hit, but power. He was feared. In the late innings, they didn't want to give him anything to hit. He was a devastating hitter. He had such a great eye. I could see that from center field.

"When he hit those high, fly balls — those were the ones that would go out for home runs. His line drives were hit so hard, they sunk. I remember one he hit right at me. I ran in for it and the ball had so much topspin, it handcuffed me. I put my glove one way and the ball went another."

WILLIAMS VS. DIMAGGIO
CAREER COMPARISON

WILLIAMS		DIMAGGIO
19	YEARS	13
2,292	GAMES PLAYED	1,736
7,706	AT-BATS	6,821
2,654	HITS	2,214
.344	AVERAGE	.325
525	DOUBLES	389
71	TRIPLES	131
521	HOME RUNS	361
1,839	RBI	1,537
18	ALL-STAR APPEARANCES	13

Williams always agreed — he was a better hitter than DiMaggio.

"In my heart, I've always felt I was a better hitter than Joe, which was always my first consideration," said Williams, whose lifetime batting average was .344 to DiMaggio's .320.

But he thought DiMaggio was a better ballplayer.

"I have to say he was the greatest baseball player of our time," said Williams. "He could do it all. He was a better fielder. A better thrower. Everything he did was stylish. He ran gracefully, he fielded gracefully, he hit with authority and style.

"Even when he missed, Joe looked good. It is also true, of course, that in his 13 years with the Yankees, they won 10 pennants. That has to be a factor."

They didn't go out to dinner together, but for years they shadowed one another, wherever they went. In 1941, DiMaggio hit in 56 straight games. Williams hit .406. In 1947, Williams won the Triple Crown. DiMaggio won the Most Valuable Player Award by one vote.

"It was an issue at the time," said DiMaggio. "We both had good years. I think at the time they took into consideration if your team won the pennant. I made

the remark at the time that if the MVP voting had finished in a tie, I would have been happy."

Who couldn't compare them? Cab drivers did. Kids with baseball cards did. Red Sox owner Tom Yawkey and Yankees owner Dan Topping did.

In 1947, they nearly traded them for each other.

"The feeling was that a right-handed power hitter like Joe was made for Fenway Park, with that short fence in left field, and I was better suited for Yankee Stadium, with right field so handy," Williams said in his autobiography, My *Turn at Bat*,

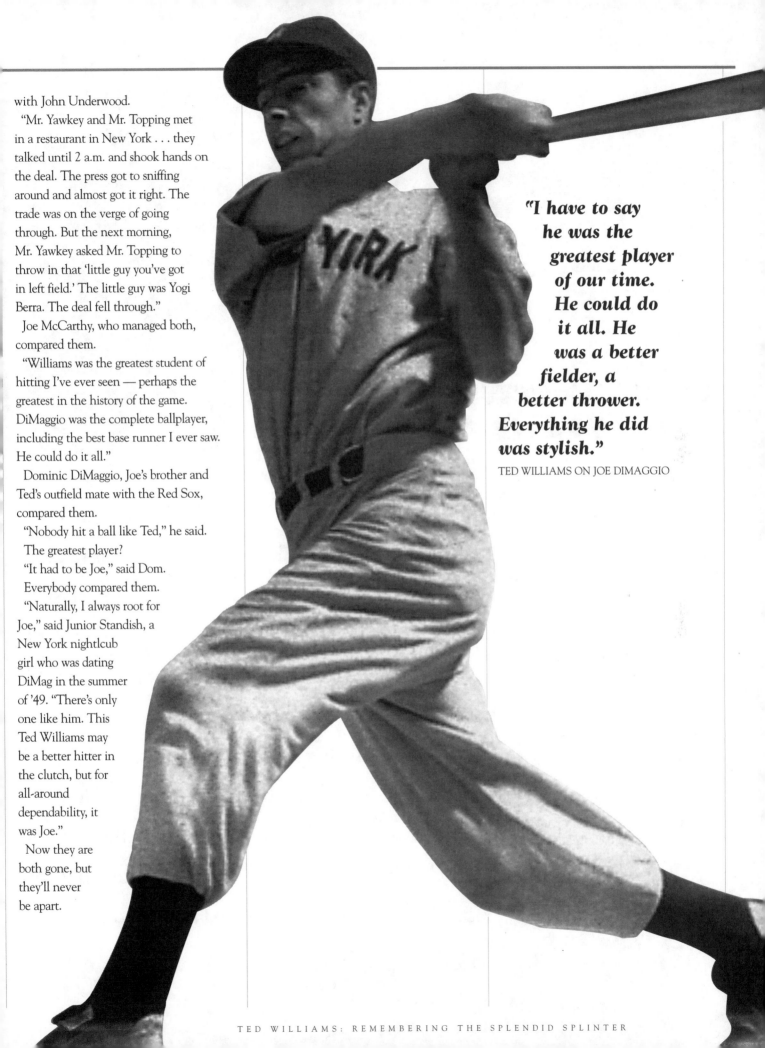

with John Underwood.

"Mr. Yawkey and Mr. Topping met in a restaurant in New York . . . they talked until 2 a.m. and shook hands on the deal. The press got to sniffing around and almost got it right. The trade was on the verge of going through. But the next morning, Mr. Yawkey asked Mr. Topping to throw in that 'little guy you've got in left field.' The little guy was Yogi Berra. The deal fell through."

Joe McCarthy, who managed both, compared them.

"Williams was the greatest student of hitting I've ever seen — perhaps the greatest in the history of the game. DiMaggio was the complete ballplayer, including the best base runner I ever saw. He could do it all."

Dominic DiMaggio, Joe's brother and Ted's outfield mate with the Red Sox, compared them.

"Nobody hit a ball like Ted," he said.

The greatest player?

"It had to be Joe," said Dom.

Everybody compared them.

"Naturally, I always root for Joe," said Junior Standish, a New York nightlcub girl who was dating DiMag in the summer of '49. "There's only one like him. This Ted Williams may be a better hitter in the clutch, but for all-around dependability, it was Joe."

Now they are both gone, but they'll never be apart.

"I have to say he was the greatest player of our time. He could do it all. He was a better fielder, a better thrower. Everything he did was stylish."

TED WILLIAMS ON JOE DIMAGGIO

TED GOES TO WAR

WILLIAMS SERVED FIVE YEARS IN THE PRIME OF HIS CAREER

David Cataneo

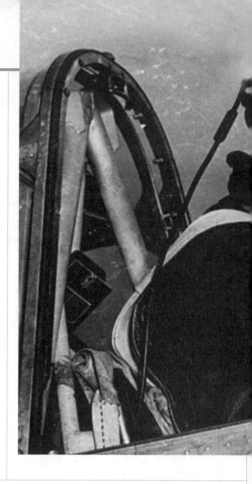

On April 30, 1952, Ted Williams made a farewell speech at Fenway Park, hit a home run in his final at-bat, and left for the Marines. Red Sox fans hated to see him go. Williams wasn't crazy about it, either. "He was what I call a reluctant warrior," Tom Ross said from his home in Niceville, Fla., reminiscing about flying fighter jets with Williams in the Korean War. "Flying was something he was doing because he had to. He was a guy who was caught up in the times and thrown into it. But he did his duty, and he didn't make a big deal out of it. I think we all respected him for that."

and it was good publicity to roust a famous reserve out of the Red Sox' outfield.

"To be truthful, I think he resented it," said Joe Locker, who was flying night fighters in Korea when he became friendly with Williams.

But unlike other duties he resented — playing the outfield and talking to the press, to name two — Williams put all his energies into flying. When he wanted to become a better hitter, he talked hitting with Rogers Hornsby and anyone else who could help. When he wanted to become a better aviator, he talked flying with John Glenn, his operations commander in Korea, and anyone else who could help.

"He asked questions all the time," said Jim Stehle, 74, of Miami, who was stationed with Williams at airbase K-3 in Korea. "He was soaking it all in.

"Determined. You bet your ass he was."

Williams had all the right stuff to be a top pilot: 20-10 eyesight, first-rate reflexes and generous portions of cockiness and ego. During World War II, he declined opportunities to ride out the war on service baseball teams. He wanted to win a pair of wings because they were hard to get, which was the perfect lure for his defiant personality. It turned out to be easier than hitting .400 — he set gunnery records, scored high on reaction tests and graduated at the top of his class.

"You've probably read that he could read the seams on a baseball," Stehle said. "He could read anything from the air, too. He wasn't just an ordinary pilot who had to be over there. He was a goddamn good one."

Which was amazing, given his experience. Many of his Marine colleagues thought Williams was rushed through the difficult transition from propeller planes to jets. Williams, who confided to several friends before he shipped out that he expected to be killed in Korea, thought so, too.

"He enjoyed flying, but he felt he didn't have enough time," Locker said. "I have to agree with him. He didn't have enough

THUMBS UP: After being sworn into the Marines after the 1942 season, Ted Willaims spent World War II as a flight instructor itching to see combat. He was awaiting his orders at Pearl Harbor when the war ended in August 1945. Williams returned to the Red Sox in 1946. He was recalled to the Marines in 1952 and flew 39 combat missions during the Korean War over the next two years. 'He wasn't just an ordinary pilot who had to be over there,' said Jim Stehle, who was stationed with Williams in Korea. 'He was a goddamn good one.'   *HERALD FILE PHOTO*

Williams had served three years in the Marines during World War II, most of the time as a flight instructor itching to get into combat. He was at Pearl Harbor awaiting orders to finally get into action in China when the war ended in August 1945.

By the summer of 1952, he wasn't so itchy anymore. Williams was 33 years old, married with a young daughter and hadn't piloted a plane in eight years when the Marines recalled him and about 1,100 other senior lieutenants and captains. The war was dragging into its third year, the Marines were short of trained pilots,

TRACKING THE SOX: Ted Williams reads a copy of the *Stars & Stripes* newspaper in Korea in 1953.

HERALD FILE PHOTO

radio went dead, and his control panel lit up like a Christmas tree. "The F-9 had a centrifugal flow engine," Glenn once recalled. "And when it got hit and caught on fire, the tail would blow off almost every time. So the standard orders were that if you had a fire in the back of the plane you were to eject immediately. Ted was trailing smoke and fire. People were yelling at him over the radio, 'Get out!' But his radio was out, and he couldn't see all this going on behind him."

"He got a tailful of arrows," said Ross, who was also on the mission. "He was streaming fuel. He was running out of fluid at a rapid rate." Pilots all over Korea were tuned into the drama.

"I happened to be on that mission," Jerry Coleman said from his San Diego home. The Marines had recalled him from the Yankees' infield to fly Corsairs in Korea. "All of a sudden, we heard this desperate mayday situation. A pilot had a burning pipe. We didn't know who it was."

Lt. Larry Hawkins pulled up next to Williams, tried to signal to him the severity of the fire and guided him to the nearest airfield. Williams lined up his approach and tried to slow the plane, but nothing worked. His wheels were jammed in the up position, and his dive brakes and flaps were useless. He screeched in at 200 mph, bellied onto the Marsden matting, and skidded for 2,000 feet.

"I thought I would never stop," Williams once recalled.

"Why it didn't blow, I don't know," Coleman said.

When the plane, which Williams later estimated had 20 or 30 seconds worth of fuel left, finally stopped, it erupted in complete flames.

time in jets to go over there."

"I always thought he was thrown into the situation long before he should have been," Ross said. "I think the Marine Corps might be faulted for putting him into that situation, for publicity purposes or whatever reason. It's to his credit that Ted did what he did."

Williams made himself a good pilot, which was clear on his first combat mission on the morning of Feb. 16, 1953. Capt. Williams was piloting an F-9 Panther in a strike against a troop encampment near Kyomipo, south of Pyongyang. Pulling off the target, Williams' plane was hit by ground fire. His control stick vibrated, his

PROJECTED CAREER STATS

	CAREER TOTAL	CAREER RANK	PROJECTED TOTAL	PROJECTED RANK
GAMES	2,292	63rd	3,017	6th
AT BATS	7,706	100th	10,149	12th
RUNS	1,798	13th	2,301	1st
HITS	2,654	48th	3,496	6th
DOUBLES	525	19th	692	5th
TRIPLES	71	—	—	93
HOME RUNS	521	10th	686	3rd
EXTRA BASE HITS	1,117	10th	1,471	2nd by 6
RBIs	1,839	11th	2,242	2nd
TOTAL BASES	4,884	13th	6,433	2nd
WALKS	2,019	2nd	2,659	1st
STRIKEOUTS	709	—	934	99th
STOLEN BASES	24	—	32	—
GRAND SLAMS	17	—	22	2nd
AVERAGE	.344	6th	—	—
ON BASE PCT.	.483	1st	—	—
SLUGGING PCT.	.634	2nd	—	—

Had Ted Williams played in the 727 games he missed while in the Marines his career totals and all-time rank would be as shown in this chart.

SOURCE - HITTER, THE LIFE AND TURMOILS OF TED WILLIAMS, BY ED LINN

"I didn't go down with him," Ross said. "Bill McGraw went in with him, and I remember after Ted got the bird down, I heard Bill say, 'You'd better get out of there, Ted. It might blow.' "

Williams popped the canopy, plopped onto the airstrip, picked himself up and ran. And the plane blew.

"I have one or two pictures of that airplane," Stehle said. "There wasn't much left of it."

Williams insisted on flying a mission the next day.

"Ted wasn't the kind of guy who would admit to being frightened or concerned," Ross said. "Of course, he was a little shook up about things like that. We all were. I know when I was shot down shortly after that, I was concerned. But you just didn't talk about it."

Williams flew 39 missions before a chronic ear ailment cut short his tour. He was shipped home and discharged July 10, 1953. He was 34. The war didn't take his life, but it did take something precious from him.

"The goddamn government took four or five years out of his life," Stehle said. "Could you imagine what he could have done with those years? Even if he had had just mediocre years?"

You could add it up. Williams was 24 whe he joined the service after the 1942 season (during which he batted .356 with 36 home runs.) He missed 1943, '44, and '45. He was 33 when he was recalled into the Marines and missed virtually all of the 1952 and '53. So he missed five prime seasons. He averaged more than 32 home runs in his non-war years from 1941-57 and finished with 521. So Hitler, Tojo and Harry Truman conceivably cost him at least 160 home runs and a shot at Babe Ruth's 714.

His wartime colleagues, many of whom became his lifelong friends, remember Williams as a great pilot and a great Marine buddy.

"The first time we met was at Cherry Point," Stehle said. "We were drawing our equipment. He said, 'Where the hell you

going, Bush?' He called everybody 'Bush.' Except generals. He didn't call generals 'Bush.' I'm not sure if he would call the Pope 'Bush.'

"I don't think you could find a better pilot. And he was a terrific guy. I don't think there's anyone I would have rather trusted my life to than Ted Williams."

But they also remember a colleague with his mind totally focused on flying, but his heart elsewhere.

"We used to get up at 3 o'clock in the morning, have a light breakfast, have a briefing and take off on a mission," Ross said. "The idea was to be over the bomb line at very first light and attack the Chinese vehicles on the main supply route.

"We'd get back to K-3 at about 6:30 and have breakfast. I remember this very vividly. I'd come into the room and there'd be 12 pilots around the table, having their second or third cups of coffee. And there'd be Ted Williams, regaling them with stories about baseball. He loved to talk about baseball."

GLOVE
WASN'T A FIRST
LOVE

David Cataneo

Ted Williams was more intense about his hitting - and his fishing and his flying and his arguing with newspapermen - than he was about his fielding. But he wasn't a bad fielder, or a harmful fielder, or even a designated hitter before his time. "He was an average major league fielder," Birdie Tebbetts, who played against Williams as a Tigers catcher from 1936-47 and with Williams as a member of the Red Sox from 1947-50, once said. "He was as good as he could be. And better than he'll ever get credit for."

His lifetime fielding average in left field was .974. For comparison: His immediate successor in left field, Carl Yastrzemski, was .981 in left, Jim Rice .980. Williams' scouting report: Great hit, OK field.

"I think, without being overly critical, he was adequate," Chuck Stevens, who played first base for the St. Louis Browns in the '40s, once said.

The unfair rap on Williams afield was that he didn't care about it. He didn't care about it as much as he did his hitting, but that's like saying Michelangelo cared more about his painting than his bocci.

He had his lapses in the field.

"Ted Williams was the greatest hitter I ever saw. But he was the only guy I ever remember raising my voice to in the clubhouse," Rudy York, who played with the Red Sox near the end of his career, in 1946-47, once recalled. "That was in 1946, when we were going for the pennant. It seemed to me that Ted was slow going after a hit in the outfield and a run scored. So in the clubhouse, I had a few things to say to him. Ted took it in the right spirit."

But he worked at it.

"During batting practice, he wanted to catch every fly ball hit to left field," Matt Batts, a Red Sox catcher in the '50s, once recalled. "When he was out there, he wanted to get every ball hit out there. He worked at it. I don't ever remember him dropping a ball. I don't know why people rap him for his fielding. He wasn't no Joe DiMaggio, but he was a fine fielder."

Williams wasn't fast enough to be a great fielder, but he made himself better in left field by putting his mind to it. He was a better hitter because he studied pitchers' tendencies and remembered them. He was a better fielder because he studied the quirks of the left-field wall at Fenway and remembered them.

"I'll guarantee you, if you hit that wall out there, he held you to a single," Batts said. "He could play that darn wall. I think he was probably the best left fielder at Fenway Park that you could have. He knew that wall as well as anybody."

Williams also utilized some trickery.

"He used to fake catches with runners on base — make the runner think he was going to catch the ball," said Boo Ferriss, a Red Sox pitcher from 1945 through 1950. "He'd be on the warning track, leaning against The Wall, popping his hand in his glove. That would hold the runner up."

But mostly he used his head, given his limited range and Dominic DiMaggio's presence in center field.

"He'd say, 'C'mon over, Dom. You can get it. C'mon over and get it, Dom,'" Ferriss said. "And Dom usually got it, too."

I'VE GOT IT: The Red Sox' lanky outfielder, Ted Williams, leaps and grabs a line drive during a spring training session on March 14, 1939, in Florida. AP PHOTO

"I don't know why people rap him for his fielding. He wasn't no Joe DiMaggio, but he was a fine fielder."
MATT BATTS, FORMER TEAMMATE

THIS RUN WAS PRECIOUS

INSIDE-THE-PARK
RIP CLINCHES PENNANT

David Cataneo

Ted Williams wasn't the greatest base runner who ever lived. A quick sampling of all-time slowpokes shows the not-so-splendid sprinter had just five more stolen bases lifetime than Harmon Killebrew, four more than Boog Powell, and one fewer than Roy Campanella. But one season, Williams' speed won the Sox a pennant. "I was just talking to somebody about that the other day," Boo Ferriss, who pitched for the Red Sox from 1945 through 1950, once recalled. "It was one of the greatest sights I ever saw."

It happened on Friday the 13th in September 1946, when the Red Sox were trying to nail down their first pennant since World War I. They had blown four straight chances to clinch the crown. Now they were in Cleveland to play the Indians at League Park, and starter Tex Hughson told his Red Sox teammates, "get me a run and we'll win."

Williams was a good candidate to get the run, because the Indians started a right-hander, Red Embree, and League Park had a tantalizing short porch in right.

"The right-field fence was just behind first base," said Ferriss. "It was short."

Williams stepped to the plate in the first inning. Cleveland manager Lou Boudreau's Williams Shift was on — the Indians' defense was packed into the right side of the field, with only the left fielder, stationed just behind the normal shortstop position, to guard the left.

Williams hated to hit to the opposite field as much as he hated to wear neckties. But he also hated to see Tom Yawkey's celebratory champagne get warm.

Williams, who had enough bat control to rope fouls into the stands when he wanted to bean a heckler, cracked a hit.

"It was right down the left-field line," said Ferriss.

And the race was on.

People who loved Williams dearly are always delicate about his speed.

"He was an adequate base runner," former Red Sox catcher Matt Batts once said.

He wasn't deathly slow. His grounded-into-double plays average for his career was 14 — about the same as Pee Wee Reese, Rod Carew, Jackie Robinson and Joe DiMaggio, and far fewer than Jim Rice.

"He didn't have much speed," Ferriss said. "But he knew how to run the bases. He didn't get picked off a lot or anything."

But he wasn't fast. And there he was, as the ball rolled to the fence, trying to leg out an inside-the-park home run.

"That was some sight, seeing him lope around the bases, those long legs pumping," said Ferriss, still trying to stifle a laugh 49 years later. "He looked like he was running for his life."

He was running for a pennant.

"We were all hollering, 'Come on, Ted! Come on, Ted!' " Ferriss said. "We were also a little wild-eyed. Imagine. Ted Williams going for an inside-the-park home run. In League Park. He could have hit one off his fists and hit it out of there."

Williams slid across the plate as the throw arrived wide on the third base side.

"He was clapping his hands and jumping around the way he did," Ferriss said. "He was also a little tired."

The final score: Red Sox 1, Indians 0. They broke out the champagne.

"He got the clincher," said Ferriss, as if it were still hard to believe, "with his legs."

Williams hit 521 lifetime homers. "It was the hardest," he once said of his mad dash in Cleveland. "I had to run."

MAGIC MOMENT: Ted Williams scores with an inside-the-park home run on Sept. 13, 1946, to clinch the pennant. PHOTO COURTESY OF GEORGE SULLIVAN

A REAL
PITCH
MAN

Ted Williams was 21 years old and bragging "what a loss to baseball that I haven't followed up on my pitching."

So on Aug. 24, 1940, as the Tigers were spanking the Red Sox at Fenway Park in the eighth inning, manager Joe Cronin called Williams in from left field and put the ball in his hand.

A pitcher-outfielder in high school, Williams was game. And in two innings, he allowed one run on three hits. He shocked Tigers slugger Rudy York with a sweeping, side-arm curveball that York took for a called strike three.

"He pitched against me," Birdie Tebbetts, former Tigers and Sox catcher, once recalled. "He said he struck me out. I say I got a double."

PITCHING IN: Making a relief appearance, Ted Williams gets set to release the ball on Aug. 24, 1940, against the Detroit Tigers. It was Williams' only major-league pitching performance. PHOTO COURTESY OF GEORGE SULLIVAN

STAR POWER

TREMENDOUS HOME RUNS HIGHLIGHTED TED'S ALL-STAR GAME HEROICS

Steve Buckley

An elderly woman answered the phone at the Lucedale, Miss., home of former major-league pitcher Claude Passeau. After a simple request to speak to him, she said: "Hold the line." Then she was heard saying: "Claude, there's a man from Boston who wants to talk to you about the home run you gave up to Ted Williams."

MIDSUMMER MOMENT: A jubilant Ted Williams is greeted by Joe Dimaggio (5) after his three-run game-winning home run in the ninth inning of the 1941 All-Star Game at Briggs Stadium in Detroit. In a May 2000 interview, Williams called it 'a magical home run.'

PHOTO COURTESY OF
NEW ENGLAND SPORTS MUSEUM

And so it goes for Claude Passeau, who forever will be remembered as the pitcher who served up a three-run, ninth-inning, game-winning home run to Williams in the 1941 All-Star Game. Passeau won 162 games during a 13-year big-league career, yet whenever anyone calls the house it's understood that it has something to do with Williams' homer.

Williams played in 18 All-Star games during his career. He hit four All-Star home runs, including two in the 1946 game at Fenway Park, one of them his famous monster shot off Rip Sewell's reknowned eephus pitch. Yet baseball historians agree — and Williams always agreed right along with them — that his shot off Passeau was the biggest All-Star home run of his career. In an interview with a San Diego television station in

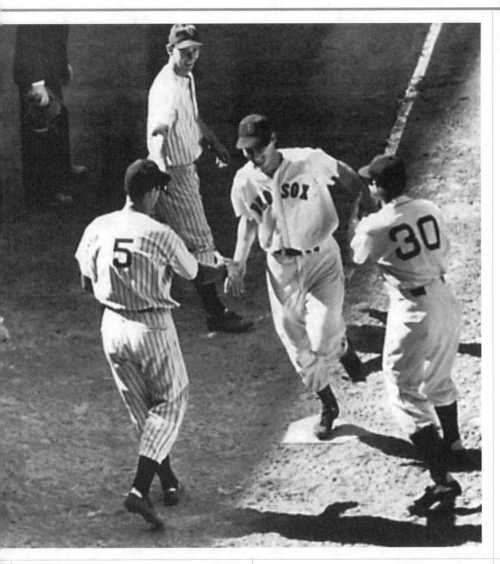

NO ONE REMEMBERS: Claude Passeau (top above) struck out Ted before giving up his homer. *HERALD* FILE PHOTO

FRONT PAGE: Williams' All-Star home run was big news in the *Herald* on July 9, 1941. (above) *HERALD* FILE PHOTO

May 2000, Williams called it "a magical home run."

It is important to understand that the All-Star Game in those days was taken a lot more seriously, by players as well as fans, than it is today. These days, players beg out of the All-Star Game for all kinds of reasons. In Ted's day, that simply wasn't done. If you were picked to participate, you did.

The 1941 All-Star Game was played at Briggs Stadium in Detroit. Passeau, a Chicago Cubs right-hander, was the fourth National League pitcher of the day, following starter Whit Wyatt and relievers Paul Derringer and Bucky Walters. By the ninth inning, the NL held a 5-3 lead, thanks in part to a pair of home runs by Arky Vaughan.

Passeau had already worked two innings. He struck out Williams when he faced

him in the eighth inning.

In an interview in November 2000, Passeau, 91 years old, said he never was able to figure out why he worked the ninth inning.

"I'm not making excuses, but it's just one of those things," Passeau said. "Carl Hubbell was warming up in the bullpen and he was only one of the greatest pitchers of the time, even though he was at the end of his career. Bill McKechnie was our manager, and he said to me, 'Oh, you've just been throwing batting practice to those guys. Go out and pitch the ninth.' "

Soon, there was trouble. The bases were loaded with one out and up came Joe DiMaggio. The Yankee Clipper hit a hard grounder to shortstop Eddie Miller, who fed the ball to Billy Herman. If the double play was completed, the game was over. Herman's throw to first

baseman Frank McCormick was wide of the bag. It was 5-4, two out, two on . . . and Williams at the plate.

Williams fouled off the first pitch. He took the next two pitches, both balls.

What did Passeau throw Williams on 2 and 1? Even in 2000, Passeau insisted he threw Williams "a slider, high and inside," though the pitch was a rarity in those days. Whatever it was, Williams caught all of it, sending a shot deep to right field and into the upper deck.

Newsreel footage of the home run shows a jubilant Williams clapping his hands twice as he runs up the first-base line. He skips past first base and completes his tour of the bases quickly but with his head down. He brushes away fans as he passes third and is greeted with a handshake from DiMaggio at home plate.

Williams, just 22 years old, gave the American League a breathtaking 7-5 victory over the NL.

"Nobody ever calls to ask me how I struck out Ted Williams in the eighth inning of the 1941 All-Star Game," Passeau said, chuckling. "They only want to know what happened in the ninth inning."

Said his son, Claude Passeau Jr.: "Dad had a very fine career pitching for a lot of bad teams. But if he has to be remembered for giving up a home run, we're glad that it was a home run to the greatest hitter of all time."

HE DOES IT AGAIN

Boston was a truly hopping city in 1946. The war was over. James Michael Curley was back in the mayor's office. A young but well-heeled veteran named John F. Kennedy was knocking on doors in Eastie, Charlestown and Cambridge in his first bid for elective office.

And then there were the Red Sox. With the likes of Williams, Dom DiMaggio, Bobby Doerr and Johnny Pesky picking up right where they left off following military service, the '46 Red Sox emerged as the top team in the AL.

How appropriate, then, that after a one-year absence, the All-Star Game returned in 1946 and was played at Fenway Park. And how appropriate that Williams, the Red Sox' greatest star, put his personal stamp on the game.

A packed house of 34,906 attended the '46 All-Star Game, played on the afternoon of July 9. And it was a joyous day for Red Sox fans, as Teddy Ballgame went 4 for 4, including two home runs, to power the AL to a 12-0 victory. His five RBIs set an All-Star record.

While the 1941 home run remains a more significant home run in hardball lore, the 1946 shot off Sewell is better remembered by oldtime Red Sox fans not only because the game was played at Fenway, but

HOME SWEET HOMER: When Rip Sewell decided "to entertain the fans" with his eephus pitch, Ted Williams provided the biggest entertainment for Fenway fans by slugging it out.

AP PHOTO

because of the novelty of the eephus pitch.

Though the game already was a rout by the time Williams connected for his second home run of the day, it nonetheless became one of the most memorable homers in Fenway history. Pitching for the NL by the eighth inning was Truett Banks "Rip" Sewell, a Pittsburgh Pirates right-hander who gained a measure of fame with his so-called eephus pitch.

The eephus was a novelty, a high, blooping pitch that frustrated some NL hitters. Williams couldn't wait to take a

cut on one of those pitches, and Sewell accommodated him. Sewell gave up four runs in his one inning, three of them coming across on Teddy Ballgame's second homer of the game. Sewell later said he threw the pitch "to entertain the fans." Williams also homered in the fourth inning, drilling a 1-2 pitch from Kirby Higbe of the Brooklyn Dodgers into the center-field bleachers.

Williams was one of six Red Sox players to appear before the hometown fans in the '46 All-Star Game. The others? Most

BLOOPING PITCH: Rip Sewell's eephus pitch fooled some NL hitters, but not Williams.
HERALD FILE PHOTO

HERALDING HISTORY: Williams' heroics landed on the *Herald* front page July 10, 1946.

TED WILLIAMS IN ALL-STAR GAMES

Year	Team	POS	AVG	AB	R	H	2B	3B	HR	RBI	BB	SO	E
1940	Bos.	LF	.000	2	0	0	0	0	0	0	1	0	0
1941	Bos.	LF	.500	4	1		1	0	1	4	1	1	1
1942	Bos.	LF	.50	4	0	1	0	0	0	0	0	0	0
1946	Bos.	LF	1.000	4	4	4	0	0	2	5	1	0	0
1947	Bos.	LF	.500	4	0		1	0	0	0	0	1	0
1948	Bos.	PH	—	0	0	0	0	0	0	0	1	0	0
1949	Bos.	LF	.000		1	0	0	0	0	0	1		0
1950	Bos.	LF	.50	4	0	1	0	0	0	1	0	1	0
1951	Bos.	LF	.333	3	0	1	0	1	0	0	1	1	0
1954	Bos.	PH/LF	.000		1	0	0	0	0	0	1		0
1955	Bos.	LF	.333	3	1	1	0	0	0	0	1	0	0
1956	Bos.	LF	.50	4	1	1	0	0	1		0	1	0
1957	Bos.	LF	.000	3	1	0	0	0	0	0	1	0	0
1958	Bos.	PH/LF	.000		0	0	0	0	0	0	0	1	0
1959	Bos.	PH	—	0	0	0	0	0	0	0	1	0	0
1959	Bos.	LF	.000	3	0	0	0	0	0	0	0	0	0
1960	Bos.	PH	1.000	1	0	0	0	0	0	0	0	0	0
1960	Bos.	PH	1.000	1	0	1	0	0	0	0	0	0	0
TOTALS				304	46	10	14	2	1	4	12	11	9	1

of them are easy to remember.

"Yes, I was there," said Pesky. "I went 0 for 2 and made an error, but nobody noticed. When it was over, everyone was talking about Ted."

A BAD BREAK

No story about Williams' All-Star exploits would be complete without mentioning the 1950 All-Star Game at Chicago's old Comiskey Park. Williams went 1 for 4 in the game, a 14-inning, 4-3 NL victory, but it was a fielding play in the first inning that haunted him for the rest of his career.

In the bottom of the first, Pirates slugger Ralph Kiner sent a deep fly to left center that Williams snared with a nice over-the-shoulder catch while on the run. As Williams neared the wall, he reached out with both hands and braced himself. He didn't know it at the time, but upon impact Williams broke his left elbow.

He remained in the game until the eighth inning. He had an RBI single and also hit a deep fly of his own that Kiner hauled in. Williams also made yet another fine catch

of a Kiner smash. Yet the damage was done.

The surgery was performed two days after the game, on July 13 at Sancta Maria Hospital in Cambridge. Williams did not return to the lineup until Sept. 15. Though he appeared in only 89 games in 1950, he still managed to drive in 97 runs.

Yet it was the first time in Williams' career he didn't drive in at least 100 runs, ending a streak of eight straight 100-RBI seasons. Throughout the rest of his career, he had 100 RBIs in only one more season, 126 in 1951.

A STAR AMONG STARS

TED STOLE THE SHOW AT THE MIDSUMMER CLASSIC IN '99

Karen Guregian

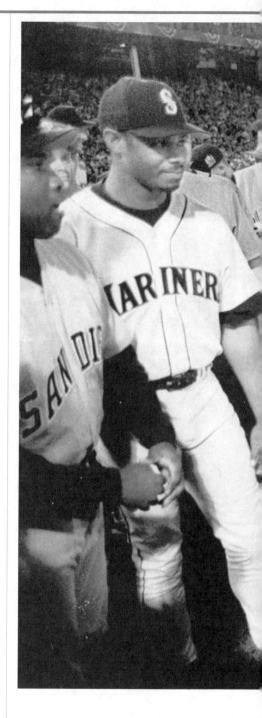

As far as All-Star moments go, Ted Williams authored what many consider the greatest one of them all when he slugged a two-out walk-off three-run homer in the bottom of the ninth inning in the 1941 midsummer classic at Briggs Stadium in Detroit. Almost six decades later, Teddy Ballgame supplied an even better entry into the greatest moment category. And he did it by merely showing up in a golf cart.

SPLENDID MOMENT: All-Stars past and present greet Ted Williams.

Red Sox pitcher Pedro Martinez may have dazzled the crowd by punching out the side in the first inning of that memorable 1999 All-Star Game at Fenway Park, but that was just icing on the cake.

The 80-year-old Williams had already warmed up the crowd shortly before the game started. He made an entrance to beat all entrances, lighting the torch for the final All-Star Game of this century.

Riding shotgun in a golf cart driven by longtime Sox employee Al Forester, Williams emerged from a huge red curtain covering the doorway under the center-field bleachers.

With 34,187 teary-eyed fans applauding wildly, Forester slowly steered Williams around the ballpark. It was one last lap for the ages, as the Sox legend waved his white cap to the crowd.

Traveling past the right field bullpens, Pesky's Pole, the first-base dugout, home plate and third base, Forester finally pulled Williams to a stop at the pitcher's mound.

It was here that an indelible picture was left in our minds, as the Splendid Splinter was immediately surrounded by both All-Star squads, along with thirty or so players who made the list of top 100 ballplayers in baseball history.

ROYAL WELCOME: Ted Williams tips his hat to the crowd as Sox employee Al Forester drives him into Fenway Park. *HERALD STAFF PHOTO*

From former greats like Willie Mays, Stan Musial, Bob Feller and Hank Aaron, to the day's current superstars like Mark McGwire, Sammy Sosa, Ken Griffey Jr., and Nomar Garciaparra, the entire cast spontaneously swarmed the Hall of Famer.

They formed a giant ring around Ted's golf cart. It was the grandfather of baseball, mobbed by all of his grandchildren; the greatest hitter who ever lived, hailed by all the rest.

The scene was magical, almost mythical. And those looking around the grand old ballpark, as well as those flocked around No. 9, were hard-pressed to find a dry eye in the house.

Many of the ballplayers welled up with tears. Given the stature of the man, and the impromptu gathering at the mound, it was hard not to be emotional.

"Here you had some of the best players of all time, along with all of the best guys

"You had some of the best players of all time... We were just in awe, wanting to go over and see him."

NOMAR GARCIAPARRA ON
GREEETING TED WILLIAMS

presently playing," Garciaparra said when recalling the moment a year later, "and we were just in awe, wanting to go over and see him."

Williams chatted with several of the current-day hardball heroes — namely Garciaparra, McGwire, Sosa, Griffey Jr. Tony Gwynn and Cal Ripken Jr. — before rising out of the cart to deliver the game's ceremonial first pitch. He threw it to fellow Sox Hall of Famer Carlton Fisk.

It wasn't a strike, but octogenarian Williams, whose body had endured a stroke as well as several other ailments over the years, managed to hurl it to the plate on the fly from just in front of the pitcher's mound.

The packed house went nuts. The ovation continued long after Ted's golf cart disappeared. New England's most revered athlete put an emotional charge into the crowd, and in turn, the Fenway

faithful put a charge into him.

"I can only describe it as great," Williams said that night with respect to his reception. "It didn't surprise me all that much because I know how these fans are here in Boston. They love this game as much as any player, and Boston's lucky to have the faithful Red Sox fans. They're the best." Martinez said: "I thought the stadium was going down. I don't think there will be another like him."

McGwire said: "A lot of guys out there kind of teared up. When you see Ted Williams with tears in his eyes, it's an emotional time."

ANOTHER SPLENDID MOMENT: Ted Williams throws out the first pitch with the help of Tony Gwynn.

HERALD STAFF PHOTO

Williams did seem genuinely touched by his reception, from the fans as well as the assemblage of past and present All-Stars who broke from script to show their admiration and respect for him.

All-Star Larry Walker said at the time there were tears in Williams' eyes as each player made his way up to him. "It was rather emotional," Walker said.

"I'm a rather emotional guy, and when I got up there, tears were coming out of Ted's eyes. I kind of turned away; it almost brought tears to my eyes.

"The greatest player in the world is surrounded by more great players. It was outstanding to see. I know Ted was extremely touched by it. It was an honor to stand out in the field with him and all

But as far as pure drama goes, it's really hard to top what happened in 1999, when Williams simply showed up in a golf cart.

the greats standing around him."

McGwire said: "A lot of guys out there kind of teared up. When you see Ted Williams with tears in his eyes, it's an emotional time. What a man. He's loved in Boston. He's loved all over. When you have a chance to meet one of the best players in the game and he has tears in his eyes, it's quite special. I'm just happy he knows who I am and he talked to me."

Williams actually discussed hitting, or rather, the smell of hitting, with McGwire that night. The legend wanted to know if the home run king smelled burnt wood after he fouled off a pitch.

Williams later explained he loved to ask all the great hitters about what he typically smelled after fouling off a ball.

"Usually when I ask players about that," Williams recalled that night, "they'll look at one another like, 'What's this guy smoking now?'"

McGwire, however, didn't think Ted was off his rocker.

"I said, all the time," McGwire replied. Williams later watched a few innings of the game with his son John Henry and baseball commissioner Bud Selig in box seats near the dugout. Then he was taken to a roof box.

According to Forester, who transported Williams all over the park that night, former Bruin greats Bobby Orr and Ray

Bourque were among the dignitaries visiting the legend in the box.

"In all of my 43 years working here, that was the best," Forester said of Ted's night. "I'm not sure it can get much better than that. And it touched him. It sure did."

It touched everyone and left a memory of the late Red Sox great people won't ever forget.

Granted, there were many other dramatic moments during his playing days and others at the All-Star game. That 1941 walk-off home run came the same summer he hit .406. He hit it off Chicago Cubs pitcher Claude Passeau. With two outs and two aboard, Williams unloaded the mighty game-winning swing. The ball wound up striking the football press box high in the right-field stands.

In the two other All-Star games held at Fenway Park, The Kid also made his presence known.

In 1946, he had the best single day in All-Star history, hitting two homers and going 4 for 4 in a 12-0 rout of the National League. He also threw out the first pitch in the other previous All-Star game at Fenway in 1961.

But as far as pure drama goes, it's really hard to top what happened in 1999, when Williams simply showed up in a golf cart.

"We didn't know we were going to be around him on the mound. It was an emotional time," said Texas first baseman Rafael Palmeiro. "We had chills all over. It was very nice being up there with a legend like that, the greatest hitter of all time. I was really proud to be a part of that."

Added Texas catcher Ivan Rodriguez said: "He's a hero to us. To see him, to be close to him, it was something very special for me. And it's something that's going to be with me for the rest of my life."

TED NOT AS SPLENDID ON BENCH

THE 20TH CENTURY IS OFFICIALLY OVER

Steve Buckley

Ted Williams was regarded by many as the greatest hitter who ever lived. He was revered for his service record, which included flying 39 combat missions in Korea. An outdoorsman, he was universally praised for his fly-casting skills. But what usually gets short shrift in most biographical treatments of Ted Williams is that, from 1969 to 1972, he was a big-league manager.

Hired by Bob Short to manage the old Washington Senators in 1969, Williams inherited a team that had lost 96 games in 1968. Williams skipped the Senators to an 86-76 record in '69 – a 21-game improvement – and was named American League Manager of the Year.

Williams signed a five-year contract to manage the Senators, for which he was to have been paid $1.25 million. However, he stepped down following the fourth season, after the Senators had been moved to Texas and retooled as the Rangers. Williams' 1972 Rangers posted a 54-100 record. His total record in four years as a big-league manager was 273-364, a .429 winning percentage.

Was Williams a good manager? It all depends on how the question is posed.

"He could have been a great manager had [Bob] Short not ruined the team on him," said Joe Camacho of Fairhaven, a onetime minor-league infielder who served as Williams' bench coach for all four of the Splinter's seasons as manager. "Short must have wanted to move that team real bad, considering the moves he made."

Specifically, Camacho, now 74, cites the infamous Oct. 9, 1970 trade in which Short dealt pitcher Joe Coleman, third baseman Aurelio Rodriguez and shortstop Ed Brinkman to the Detroit Tigers in exchange for former Cy Young Award winner Denny McLain and three other players, Don Wert, Norm McRae and Elliott Maddux.

McLain went 10-22 for the Senators in 1971 and was out of baseball by 1972. Maddux hit .217 for the '71 Senators and went on to become a career journeyman. Wert hit .050 in 20 games for the '71 Senators before being released. McRae, a pitcher who had made just 22 appearances with the Tigers in 1969 and '70, never appeared in the big leagues again after the trade.

As for Coleman, Rodriquez and Brinkman, they all became stars for the Tigers, helping lead the team to the 1972 American League East title. Coleman, in fact, emerged as one of the top pitchers in the

ON WATCH: Ted Williams strikes a pose in the dugout during his years as the manager of the Washington Senators. In 1969, his rookie season, Williams was named AL Manager of the Year.

HERALD FILE PHOTO

FIRE INSIDE: Ted Williams wasn't as successful managing, finishing with a career 273-364 record.

HERALD FILE PHOTO

KID SKIPPER

WILLIAMS' MANAGERIAL RECORD						
Year	Team	Gms		L	Pct.	
1969	WAS-A	162	86	76	.531	4E
1970	WAS-A	162	70	92	.432	6E
1971	WAS-A	159	63	96	.395	5E
1972	TEX-A	154	54	100	.351	6W
TOTALS		**637**	**273**	**364**	**.429**	

American League, going 62-38 his first three seasons with the Tigers.

"Ted hated that trade, especially losing Coleman," said Camacho. "And you can't manage without players. People say Joe Torre is a great manager — and he is — but let's remember that he was fired in Atlanta and St. Louis and with the Mets and had bad records with those teams. He didn't have the players."

Another take on Ted Williams the manager was offered by Dick Billings, a former utility man who played four seasons for Williams.

"When it came to hitting, he knew more than any manager I ever played for," said Billings, who played eight years in the big leagues and now lives in the Dallas-Ft. Worth area. "But when it came to positioning infielders and moving runners along and all that stuff, he wasn't much interested. He left all that to his coaches.

"I mean, he saw that those kind of things got taken care of," Billings said, "but that was about it."

Williams was enthusiastic and dedicated in discussing the finer points of hitting with his players. But that, too, could pose a problem, given that his players lacked the Splendid Splinter's unmatched natural skills.

"He was a great guy and I had a lot of respect for him," said Billings, "but when he'd be talking to me about looking for a fastball on the inside part of the plate on 3 and 1 . . . well, you can only go so far with that. He'd be talking about waiting on that pitch, but it's something I couldn't comprehend."

The most oft-told story about Williams' managerial career involves Camacho, his faithful bench coach, and base coach Nellie Fox. It was during spring training, and Camacho and Fox got into a heated argument over the proper way to conduct a rundown drill. The two coaches argued and argued, until, finally, Williams was asked to intervene.

After listening to both men, Williams simply said, "To hell with it. Let's just hit."

Did the story really take place?

"Yes," said Camacho. "It's turned into a big fight over the years when it was really just a discussion. But that's what Ted said. He just wanted to hit."

HE'S AN AMERICAN HERO

LONGTIME FRIEND GOWDY IN AWE OF WILLIAMS ON AND OFF PLAYING FIELD

Jim Baker

You expect Curt Gowdy to join the chorus calling Ted Williams the greatest hitter ever, but the longtime friend and radio-TV voice who called more than 1,000 of his Red Sox games hardly stops there. "Ted was not only the best hitter I've ever seen, but the best fisherman," said Gowdy, who worked the Kid's 1951-60 games. "In fact, whatever he went into, he excelled at.

"I think he's an American hero. I don't know why a movie hasn't been made of his life. Most people don't know he flew right wing for John Glenn in Korea when they were in the Air Marine Corps and Glenn said he was the best jet pilot he's ever seen."

But fishing? Many knew the Splendid Splinter loved it, but Gowdy — the former host of ABC's *American Sportsman* — tells of how they hooked a lasting friendship and he found many special insights into Ted's enigmatic personality during their numerous trips to the Florida Keys.

"I came to Boston in 1951 from the Yankees, and Ted found out I liked to fly-fish," Gowdy recalled. "He'd say, 'How's the trout fishing in Wyoming (Curt's native state)?' And we became fast friends. He sort of accepted me."

Indeed. After the baseball season, they'd go to the Keys and unwind.

"We had a lot of fun together. He gives you a lot of hell, but you give it back and he likes that," Gowdy said.

How good was Williams at fishing, his second sporting passion?

"One day we were in Washington, back when the Senators were there, and he called me in my room and said, 'There's a national fly-casting exhibition here. Let's walk over.'

"I think Ted cast about three feet short of the guy who won the national championship. That's how good he was. He was not only a great friend, but he was awfully good."

Gowdy was unaware for years that Williams served with Glenn. He found out in the 1980s when the Jimmy Fund honored both.

"They had 12 of us on a stage with [host] David Hartman, but beforehand I'm in the green room and see Glenn. I didn't realize the connection and asked, 'Why are you here?'

"Glenn said when he was wing commander in Korea, 'Ted flew my right wing. He's the best I ever saw, and we've remained good friends.'

"Ted thought that in his second tour of duty at age 36-37, they were using him for publicity purposes. But he was a very fine officer—very disciplined. They said he'd be a lousy manager because he was undisciplined. But he was one of the most disciplined guys I ever met.

"People don't know what a great guy Ted is," Gowdy said. "He's very loyal to his friends. But he's volatile and a perfectionist. Everything had to be just right — like the bat a certain weight.

A DAY ON THE WATER: Curt Gowdy (left), a former Red Sox announcer, TV host and friend of Ted Williams, casts an admiring glance toward The Kid during a day of fishing.

HERALD FILE PHOTO

"And how he loves the game! He's a bright guy — ashamed he had no college education. He got mad at the writers because they wrote about his family. They wrote about his father being an alcoholic, so he started a war with the media. He didn't like guys who second-guessed him, but he'd ask, 'Why do they write about my family?'

"I told him, 'You're in a goldfish bowl.' That's the way he was, but in later years he changed. He just loved being honored at the All-Star Game here [in 1999] with the stars gathering around him at midfield. He didn't want them to leave.

"He missed two terms as a player because he was in two wars," Gowdy said. "And after he was an All-Star in, 1950 and '51, he went back for a fly at Comiskey Park and smashed an elbow. They took out three to four inches of bone.

"So one day he asked me, 'When did you first see me play?' I told him 1950-51 and he said, 'You saw me when I was great. I lost my whip after that injury. I couldn't really swing the bat around.'"

Gowdy spun another story of Williams stumbling and breaking his collarbone in 1954 spring training.

"But the best day I saw him came in a Detroit doubleheader in late May that year. He went 9 for 11 with three home runs and 9-10 RBIs.

"Here he'd never had any real spring training and yet I never saw such a show. And before the game, he told me 'I feel lousy.' Imagine that."

Money? Gowdy has an eye-opening story about that as well.

"Ted showed me his contract, and he was the highest-paid player at $125,000 a year. That became the benchmark. The owners said, 'You don't pay anyone more than Ted.' That was before free agency broke things open.

"But one year he ruptured a disk and hit only .254. [Sox owner] Tom Yawkey wanted him to retire, but he got better in the winter. Yawkey sent him a contract, but Ted sent it back, saying he didn't deserve $125,000. He wanted a $35,000 cut. He got it and signed the contract.

"Do you think the guys today would do that?"

Gowdy added: "Ted was born 30-40 years too early, but he never resented the stars who made so much more than he ever did. But he did tell me, 'I do resent the .210 hitter making $2 million.'"

Gowdy, noting how much Williams liked Nomar Garciaparra, said he always tried to help hitters — and how that bothered Yawkey and Joe Cronin when he gave tips to opposing stars.

"Yawkey and Cronin used to give him hell. Al Kaline and Mickey Mantle used to go to him for advice and Yawkey would say, 'Why are you helping the opposition?' He'd answer: 'Because I can help the game. People come to see a hitter. You can tell by the roar when you're two blocks from the park.'"

BEST FRIEND LEAVITT CRACKED TED'S FACADE

Stephen Harris

Ted Williams remained an imposing figure to the end, but through his final couple of decades he was a benevolent old softy compared to the terror he'd been during his playing days.

Yet even back then, when he'd held the upper hand in an ongoing war with Boston's sports media, there was one sportswriter he viewed differently from all others: his close friend for more than half a century, outdoors columnist Ralph William "Bud" Leavitt of the *Bangor Daily News*.

LEAVITT: Ted's best pal

How did Bud Leavitt, who died Dec. 20, 1994, after a long fight with cancer, crack Williams' hard facade? Two ways: He knew plenty about hunting and fishing, two of the Splendid Splinter's true loves, and he more than held his own against Williams' biting wit.

"He would come right back at Ted," former Red Sox great Bobby Doerr once said of Leavitt. "If you argued with Ted a little bit, he'd admire you for it."

One can only imagine the verbal exchanges the pair must have had during their many fishing and hunting expeditions throughout the U.S. and Canada. The humorous rapport was obvious in the series of 18 television commercials Williams and Leavitt made for J.J. Nissan bread. The television exposure made Leavitt familiar to fans everywhere, but as he learned, not nearly as famous as Williams.

In a 1992 conversation with Bill Parillo of the *Providence Journal*, Leavitt told of two fishing trips he made with Williams to Anchorage, Alaska. Leaving the airport on the first trip, they were stopped by two strangers.

"Eskimos, I believe," Leavitt said. "We're ready to go, but this one guy grabs me and whispers `Hey, is that Ted Williams?' And I said, `As a matter of fact, it is.' The other guy runs off to get a piece of paper and a pencil."

So there's Williams, 5,000 miles away from Boston, signing autographs for two Eskimos.

"Ted," Leavitt said, "you can't hide."

"We were on another flight to Anchorage," Leavitt said. "Again, it was to do with some fishing. It was a big 747 and it was bound for Tokyo. Ted and I are sitting in the back, and he's trying to catch some sleep. But pretty soon, this elderly Japanese gentleman walks down the aisle, bows and asks me, `Is that Ted Williams?'

"I nod, and he pulls out an autograph book and a pen. Ted signs and the guy bows again. The next thing we know, people are getting out of their seats and there's a line clear up to the cockpit. They couldn't even serve lunch. Most of the people were Japanese."

Leavitt and Williams became friends when Leavitt occasionally covered the team at Fenway Park or during spring training.

"Bud was one of the few people Ted Williams liked," Red Sox legend Johnny Pesky once said of Leavitt. "They were very close. They fished together up and down the Eastern seaboard."

Williams "could have picked any sportswriter around to go fishing with him, but he picked Bud because he knew Bud was reliable and wouldn't go off on a tangent," Portland, Maine, outdoors columnist Gene Letourneau once said. "Bud knew what the hell he was writing about."

Doerr once said: "Ted just took a liking to him. Being a fisherman, Bud had a great outlook on life. He was just fun to be around, happy all the time." Fun to be around? Happy all the time? Doesn't sound much like the big, bad Teddy Ballgame. But maybe opposites do attract.

THE KID AND THE KIDS

GENEROUS DEEDS MADE TED'S NAME SYNONYMOUS WITH THE JIMMY FUND

Rich Thompson

HUMBLE HUMANITARIAN: Ted Williams agreed to be honored in 1953 only after he found out the proceeds would benefit the Jimmy Fund

HERALD FILE PHOTO

On Aug. 17, 1953, Ted Williams and the Jimmy Fund went public. Williams had been involved with the charity dedicated to research to cure cancer in children for years. Williams, who was a friend of famed cancer researcher and cofounder of the Jimmy Fund, Dr. Sidney Farber, had been a regular visitor at Children's Hospital, but always under the threat that the visits would stop if they were ever publicized.

So when he was first approached about a dinner to be held at the Hotel Statler in August 1953, Williams — just returned from a tour of duty as a fighter pilot in the Korean War — wanted no part of any honor. But when he was told proceeds would go to the Jimmy Fund, he quickly changed his mind.

As plans were formed, it was evident the evening would be more than a dinner for a ballplayer. It was shaping up as a world-class event. For starters, the price tag was $100 a plate — which would be about $2,500 today. The dinner was emceed by television star Ed Sullivan, who was pictured on the front page of three Boston papers the next day putting a tie around Williams' neck. And there was a 38-car parade, featuring the various stars of stage and screen who had gathered in Boston to honor Williams.

The first 25 minutes of the event were nationally televised, cameras cutting away before Williams was introduced.

TV missed a speech in which Williams summed up what baseball meant to him.

Williams was always generous with his his time when it came to the Jimmy Fund, but he never wanted his visits to the cancer wards documented. Whatever satisfaction Williams got from his time with the Jimmy Fund he tried to keep to himself.

Once, Williams was asked why he spent so much of his time visiting cancer-stricken children. The normally confident Williams appeared uncomfortable.

"Look, it embarrasses me to be praised for anything like this," he said. "The embarrassing thing is that I don't feel I've done anything compared to the people at the hospital who are really doing the important work.

"It makes me happy to think I've done a little good and I suppose that's what I get out of it. Anyway, it's only a freak of fate, isn't it, that one of those kids isn't going to grow up to be an athlete and I wasn't the one who had the cancer?"

The gala night netted more than $125,000, making it the largest single fundraiser for the Jimmy Fund at that time.

From that day forward, Williams and the Jimmy Fund were synonymous.

"He's been the single biggest draw we've ever had," Jimmy Fund executive director Mike Andrews once said of the late Red Sox legend. "He gave the Jimmy Fund the right to use his name in connection with any project we've had.

"It's been amazing," said Andrews. "Out of the blue, we'd get a check for a few thousand dollars from somewhere around the country. There'd be a note that Ted had spoken to a group and refused any money, saying, 'Send a check to the Jimmy Fund instead.'

"I can't tell you the number of checks we get every week," said Andrews, "that are made out to 'Ted Williams and the Jimmy Fund.'"

"When we ballplayers run out there on the field," he said, "we're really a bunch of boys cheating the calendar. And you fans up there in the stands — you're just kids, too, shaking off some of those grownup worries for a couple of hours and boiling right down to a simple equation like the winning and losing of a ballgame.

"The way I look at it, there is always something we can do for some youngster somewhere," said Williams. "Here, we don't have to look any further than the Jimmy Fund.

"Somehow, it strikes me that a dollar tossed into the drive is the whole American way of life in a nutshell. All the bullets and all the bombs that explode all over the world won't leave the impact, when all is said and done, of dollar bill dropped in the Jimmy Fund pot by a warm heart and a willing hand."

DOIN' THE RIGHT THING

TED GOES TO BAT FOR NEGRO LEAGUERS AT HALL OF FAME INDUCTION

Rich Thompson

The most important speech of Ted Williams' life in baseball began characteristically, with a string of undeleted expletives. Williams, of course, was elected to the Hall of Fame as soon as he was eligible and was inducted on July 25, 1966. As he moved toward the microphone on the speaker's podium in Cooperstown, someone in the crowd heckled Williams. Williams responded in kind, not knowing the mike, still steps away, was live. Ted's voice had the carry of a Tiger Woods long iron. The loudspeakers crackled with Williams' cussing. "The profanity," primly noted *Herald* reporter Henry McKenna, "tainted what was otherwise a noble day."

McKenna was wrong. No one remembers Williams' lapse into vulgarity. All baseball remembers what came next. In his formal remarks, Williams began one of the most important developments in the history of the Hall itself and arguably for the whole game as well.

It began as a standard acceptance speech. Williams thanked, somewhat ironically, the sportswriters, who'd elected him. He went on to thank his old playground director and high school coach in San Diego, Eddie Collins, the Sox scout who signed him to a contract, owner Tom Yawkey (who was present), and all of his Red Sox managers from the first half of his career.

As was (and still is) customary for a Hall acceptance speech, Williams went on to talk about what baseball had meant to him. Toward the close of his speech, he made news that eventually turned into history.

"I hope someday the names of Satchel Paige and Josh Gibson can in some way be added [to the Hall] as a symbol of the great Negro League players who are not here because they weren't given the chance," Williams said.

That one sentence began a movement. Williams wasn't the first Hall of Famer to call for inclusion of Negro League players in Cooperstown. Bob Feller, the great Indians pitcher, wrote a magazine article in 1962 urging the election of Paige, who'd been his teammate in Cleveland.

But Williams made his request in the most public way possible, in a fashion impossible for baseball's rulers to ignore. He said it to their faces, on a day when the eyes of all fans were on him. And Williams being Williams, the lords of baseball knew he wasn't about to let the matter drop.

Baseball being baseball, it wasn't until the '70s that commissioner Bowie Kuhn, under intense prodding, prevailed upon the Hall to create a Special Committee on the Negro Leagues with the power to

HALL OF FAME DAY: Ted Williams poses with Casey Stengel (center) and baseball commissioner William D. Eckert (right) on July 25, 1966.

name African-American stars to the Hall.

From 1971-77, the committee named eight such men. Paige was their first selection, Gibson their second.

Negro League players would have been named to the Hall of Fame eventually if Williams had not spoken out on their behalf. But Williams' speech, by making it an issue baseball couldn't ignore, probably moved up the timetable for those overdue honors by at least a decade.

This profound service to the history of the game was only the beginning of Williams' involvement with the Hall of Fame he graces. From 1986 on, Williams served as a member of the Veterans' Committee, the group responsible for selecting Hall of Famers not eligible to be elected by the Baseball Writers' Association.

And in the late '90s, Williams lent his credibility to the persons seeking to have Shoeless Joe Jackson elected to Cooperstown despite Jackson's involvement in the 1919 Black Sox scandal. Those folks were pretty much regarded as cranks, until Williams took their side. Jackson may never make Cooperstown, but once again, Williams gave an issue priceless attention.

Today, we see the plaques of Paige, Gibson, and their Negro League peers as Williams did in 1966, as baseball's shamed acknowledgment of the monstrous color bar that existed before 1947, and of the damage that bar did to America and the game itself.

The curses into an open mike on that July day proved yet again that Ted Williams would always say and do what he wished and devil take the consequences. The speech that came next gave the Hall of Fame reason to thank God that was Williams' way.

WILLIAMS' HALL OF FAME PLAQUE WAS A REAL BUST

Michael O'Connor

ORIGINAL: This plaque (left) was thrown out and eventually sold.

TRUE LIKENESS: Ted's second plaque (right) was more to his liking.

Nobody ever said Ted didn't have an ego.

When you've been elected to the Hall of Fame, it takes a lot of . . . something . . . to tell Hall fathers they'd better rustle up another likeness of ol' No. 9 because you don't think the first image quite captures your essence.

Of course, the folks in Cooperstown complied. What visitors see hanging in the Hall is a second bronze of the Splendid Splinter.

"Apparently, at the time he felt the first image didn't fit him properly," said Jeff Idelson, communications director for the Hall of Fame. "So they had a second plaque cast."

Idelson stressed that recasting the images of Hall members "is obviously not something we normally do."

And what about the initial, rejected, visage of Williams? Wouldn't it have become quite a collector's item?

It certainly would have - and did.

"The first casting was not destroyed, and it should have been destroyed," Idelson said. The Hall official suggested that it was simply thrown out — "and pilfered from the dumpster."

Whoever did that knew that the plaque would be valuable, Idelson said, "because it eventually got into someone's hands and found its way onto the market and has been sold."

MASTERS OF THE MONSTER

TED AND YAZ RULED FENWAY'S LEFT FIELD

Joe Giuliotti

Carl Yastrzemski was great. Ted Williams was greater. Just ask Carl Yastrzemski. "I didn't see Babe Ruth or Lou Gehrig. But I saw [Hank] Aaron, [Willie] Mays and Mickey [Mantle], who were all great hitters, but he was a step above," Yastrzemski said. "He was a step above everyone else.' Yastrzemski, who grew up on Long Island, saw Williams play many times, never dreaming that one day he would succeed the legend as the Red Sox' left fielder, then follow him into the Hall of Fame.

"He was one individual you would come to the ballpark to see hit and didn't care whether the Red Sox won or lost," he said. "He was just a great hitter, and you got your money's worth just seeing him. He was just a great hitter.

"What made him so great was his physical attributes and his mental toughness. And while I wasn't close to being as strong as him, I learned the mental part of hitting from him.

"He preached to me what I preach to our young hitters every spring: Learn the mental approach to hitting. In our talks that first spring training, he pounded the thinking part of hitting at me.

"What he taught me proved so important throughout my career. He constantly talked of learning situational hitting by making yourself mentally tough.

"He was tough mentally and that's what he pounded into me. 'Mental, mental, mental, hitting is mental,' he'd say time and time again.

"He taught me to learn pitchers. Study them and never forget how they tried to pitch you in different situations.

"We'd talk and a pitcher's name would come up. He'd say, 'This guy threw me this in 1948,' and now he's talking about a game in 1956 where the pitcher did something different to him. It was amazing. He probably remembered every pitch that was thrown to him, what it was and where it was.

"He'd stress to remember what a pitcher

LEFT FIELD LEGENDS: Carl Yastrzemski (left) and Ted Williams, talking in 1983, guarded the Green Monster (far left) for four decades.

tried to do to me and take notice of how they'd pitch me in their park and in Fenway Park, because good ones wouldn't pitch you the same.

"I learned to adjust when they threw me away in Yankee Stadium because of the short right-field porch, then came inside in Fenway and dared me to hit it 380 or 390 feet.

"He was the strongest mental individual I ever met. He taught me how important situational hitting was. 'Make yourself mentally tough,' he'd say. 'Tell yourself this guy's not going to get you out,' he'd tell me. I think we need more of that today.

"Ted also had tremendous physical attributes. I don't think anyone had physical attributes like Ted.

"I remember my first spring training, which was his last, and seeing firsthand how good he was physically. The best way I can relate it is, with his swing, if we were playing golf, I'd use a driver off the tee and Ted would take a pitching wedge and hit the ball just as far with his swing."

Yaz and Williams had more in common than hitting and left field. They both also loved to fish.

"He was the greatest hitter I saw and and also one of the greatest fishermen. I fished to relax, and he used to get on me, saying I didn't take it serious enough," Yaz said.

"My first year in spring training, I had the locker next to him and we constantly talked hitting and fishing. But it was always 99 percent hitting. He was a perfectionist when it came to hitting." Yastrzemski was so caught up as a 20-year-old meeting Williams that he tried to be like him, and in doing so — for a while — he began questioning his own ability.

"I was 20 when I came to the Red Sox and turned 21 in August, and those first three months of the season almost ruined me," he said.

"I tried to be Ted Williams, whereas I was more a Wade Boggs-type hitter when I came up.

"But following Williams, I tried to hit home runs. Getting a base hit didn't mean anything to me. Making a great defensive play didn't mean anything to me because I wanted to pop the ball out of the park like Ted. But I only weighed about 175 pounds, and right field looked like nine miles away from me at that time.

"It was a tough first three months. I was only hitting .210 but came back. I was compared to Ted when I came up, and I tried to be Ted instead of Carl Yastrzemski.

"In the second half of the season I started being myself. I just told myself nobody was ever going to be Ted Williams again, and nobody will."

> **"We constantly talked hitting and fishing. But it was always 99 percent hitting. He was a perfectionist."**
>
> CARL YASTRZEMSKI
> ON TED WILLIAMS

Hooked

FISHING WAS TED'S OTHER PASSION

Michael O'Connor

When Ted Williams wasn't swinging a bat, he was casting a line. Williams the angler was almost as well known as Williams the slugger. According to several fishing buddies of long standing, Williams truly became an avid angler upon his return from World War II and soon became a serious recreational angler. "The type of fishing he started to do, fly-fishing on the salt water, was relatively new," Florida charter boat captain Jimmy Albright, who met Williams in 1947, once recalled. "We were mostly bait-casters.

"Ted was a real good fisherman. He caught a lot of 'em, but most he turned loose. And when he was with Sears, he did as much as anybody to get people into fishing." It was the same sense of dedication and devotion that propelled him into Cooperstown for his hitting that earned him a spot in the International Game Fish Association Fishing Hall of Fame in Florida, where he did much of his angling during and after his career on the diamond.

When Williams fished, he fished, and didn't dwell on his day job, Albright once said.

"But sometimes we talked baseball. He had me come to Boston. I went to Fenway Park and went to his house. They were playing the Yankees, and Ted introduced me to all of them. That was all right.

"But on the water, we talked mainly fishing."

George Hummel, who already was an established Florida Keys guide when he and Williams linked up in 1958, became a regular fishing partner of the Splinter.

"I'm sure I was more impressed with him than he was with me," Hummel had recalled. "Ted already was a fresh water fly fishermen when he came down our way

WELL ROUNDED: Ted Williams shows off his catch after 24-hour sportsman's marathon in New Zealand. He took a 587-pound thresher shark, some rainbow trout and two red deer.

HERALD FILE PHOTO

ANOTHER FISH STORY: Ted Williams holds up his final catch before heading off to spring training in 1950.

AP PHOTO

and we got him into salt water. He heard about the [Florida] Keys when this was still more or less virgin territory."

When on a fishing trip, Williams often showed a side he dared not let Boston — or its dread press corps — witness.

"I know he was very sentimental," Hummel said. "Every year we tried to go somewhere, and we were in Costa Rica. There was this crippled woman with a little girl in her lap. Ted walked by, took out a hundred dollars and dropped it in her lap."

But Ray Crawford, editor of the IGFA magazine, said Williams always retained a touch of feistiness.

"He and I were golf partners and became pretty good friends," Crawford recalled. Of course, if Williams, who met Crawford when the two were paired for a charity golf event, knew that his partner was a Knight of the Keyboard, the two might never have connected.

"At the end of the tournament — which we won — Ted strolled into the clubhouse, feeling pretty good," recalled the former *Miami Herald* football writer and golf editor. "They put four bottles of beer in front of him and he was known to guzzle them all. He tossed down one and had started on the second when someone mentioned I was a sportswriter.

"Beer went everywhere, he was choking

and sputtering so much," Crawford recalled with a chuckle.

But Williams was always the perfectionist, and his incurable slice led him to abandon the links, Crawford said. Not so with his fishing. "When we inducted him into the Hall last year, he was the biggest name by far," the fishing magazine editor said. "He was very well known down here with fishermen. And his baseball skills were a big help."

Williams' legendary eyesight stood him in good stead on the water as well as in the batter's box, Hummel said.

"We were in the Bahamas for bonefish, and they can be hard to see [they're very fast and they prefer shallow water, which reflects the sun's glare]," he recalled. "The local guide didn't know who we were. Ted and I bet each other 50 bucks who'd get the next fish.

"Most of the time, of course, he won," Hummel said. "The guide was beside himself. He didn't see any of them. Ted just had fantastic eyes."

He also had his local angling fans, including those who were inspired to fish after attending Boston-area outdoors

shows that featured Williams and boxing legend Jack Sharkey.

"I saw him at the old Mechanics Hall," recalled Bob Lownes of Burlington, a longtime official of United Fly Tyers. "Jeez, I was about nine years old. Well, Ted was there with Sharkey and they put on some casting exhibition. That raised him higher im my estimation.

"He kind of influenced me into fly-fishing and from there into fly-tying," Lownes once said.

Fayette "Frenchy" Barrow of Winchester first saw Williams when the slugger ventured to Barrow's town to pick up an automobile.

"He used to get his cars at Hi Moody's in Winchester, and when he'd have them serviced, he stopped off at Horn Pond, fly fish down there. That's where I was and saw him for the first time. That was in the early '50s," Barrow once said.

"I love fishing; fishing was my thing. I never was a baseball fan. We never did exchange names, but he's the one got me started. He made it look so damn easy, I just had to try it," Barrow recalled. "He made everything look easy."

PICTURE PERFECT

LITTLE TED CHERISHES HIS MOMENT IN THE SUN WITH BIG TED

Steve Buckley

Ted Williams posed for thousands of photographs during his career with the Red Sox and many thousands more after his career ended. And why not? More than being the greatest hitter who ever lived, Ted Williams was also a man of unquestioned magnetism and hence a natural draw for professional photographers and shutterbugs. But while we tend to focus on the man himself when we view old photographs of Williams, what about the other people who, thanks to one frozen moment in time, find themselves forever linked with the Splendid Splinter? While sorting through hundreds of photographs in preparation for this tribute to Ted Williams, we came upon one particular photo that practically jumped out of the pile. In the photo, taken on July 28, 1955, by award-winning photographer Bruce McLean of the Boston Daily Record, we see a small boy — posing with Ted Williams.

BIG TED AND LITTLE TED: Ted Athas remembers "feeling that Ted Williams really wanted me to be comfortable" when he met the slugger in '55.

"I was too young to play, even in the pee-wee program, but I was the batboy on the team my father coached," Athas said. "The team was Pat's Supermarket. We had won the pee-wee championship that year, and our reward was a trip to Fenway Park."

PRIZED POSSESSIONS: Ted Athas, now 51, displays the baseball he caught July 28, 1955, the same day he posed for a photo with Ted Williams at Fenway Park as a four-year-old

HERALD PHOTO BY MATTHEW CAVANAUGH

The boy, decked out in a baseball uniform and black high-top sneakers, seems ill at ease, perhaps intimidated by the specter of meeting a famous baseball player. Williams, though, has a look of soft earnestness on his face, as though he genuinely wants the boy to enjoy the moment. Williams even extends his left arm and gently wraps his fingers around the boy's left elbow.

It is a magnificent photograph. But to Ted, it was just another click of the shutter. After the photo was taken, he probably headed off to the batting cage or maybe back to the clubhouse, not giving the moment any additional thought.

But what about the young boy?

A SPLENDID MEETING

The other fellow wearing a baseball uniform in that photograph is Ted Athas. He was just four years old — "To be precise, I was four and a half," he says — and had made the trip to Fenway Park that day with a group of kids from the Holyoke Youth Baseball League, which was founded by his father, Jim Athas.

"I was too young to play, even in the pee-wee program, but I was the batboy on the team my father coached," Athas said. "The team was Pat's Supermarket. We had won the pee-wee championship that year, and

our reward was a trip to Fenway Park."

Athas, who turned 50 in November and now lives in Chicopee with his wife, Joanne, and his two stepchildren, speaks with reverence about his brush with fame.

"I was a little kid from Holyoke who found himself posing for a picture with the greatest hitter who ever lived," he said. "You have no idea how many people I show that picture to, to this very day. It's a moment that I'll treasure for the rest of my life."

OK, but just how was it that this little boy from Holyoke found himself posing for a picture with Ted Williams? Before answering that question, we must revisit one of the commonly held beliefs about Ted Williams: That he hated sportswriters.

The truth is, he hated BOSTON sportswriters. Most of them, anyway. But Williams was known to be gracious and accommodating in his dealings with sportswriters from smaller cities around New England. In *Hitter: The Life and Turmoils of*

Ted Williams, the late Ed Linn wrote: "With out-of-town writers . . . Ted was usually the world's most charming citizen."

One such out-of-town writer was Bill Keating, longtime sports editor of the Holyoke *Transcript-Telegram* and a frequent chronicler of the Red Sox.

"Keats and Ted Williams got along famously," said Mike Burke, a city editor of the Springfield *Union-News* who once worked with Keating at the now-defunct *Transcript-Telegram*. "I

SNAPSHOTS TO SAVOR: Bruce Mclean, a photographer with the Boston *Daily Record*, captured Ted Athas' moment with Ted Williams.

HERALD FILE PHOTO

remember going to Boston with him in 1969, when Ted was managing the Washington Senators at Fenway Park for the first time. Ted said to all the Boston writers, 'Why can't you all be more like this guy,' pointing to Bill."

Keating, ever the solid reporter looking for a local angle, made use of that friendship when he heard that a busload of kids from the Holyoke Youth Baseball League was in attendance at Fenway Park on that Thursday afternoon in July 1955. Knowing that Jim Athas had a son named Ted and knowing that little Ted was with the group, Keating had an idea: Why not get Big Ted and Little Ted to pose together for a photograph?

"I guess he asked Ted if he'd do it, and I guess Ted said, 'Sure, why not,' " Athas said. "I don't know the specifics. I was only four and a half years old. But I do have two vivid memories of that moment. One was the feeling of being in the dugout. I remember that. The other thing I remember is having a feeling that Ted Williams really wanted me to be comfortable. I think he could sense that I was nervous. But he definitely made me less nervous than I would have been."

What's unclear is why the memorable moment was captured on film by McLean, a photographer for the Boston *Daily Record*, and not a snapper from the Holyoke *Transcript-Telegram*. Burke, Keating's protege from Holyoke, thinks he has the answer: "Even though Bill went to Fenway all the time, we didn't send a photographer. We would have used wire-service photos for the paper. I'm guessing he knew the photographer from Boston and asked him to take the picture."

It's possible that Keating and McLean were buddies, with the sportswriter from Holyoke asking the photographer from Boston to do him a favor. Then again, wouldn't Williams have been wary of posing for a photographer?

"But my father had a very good relationship with Ted," said Janet McLean of Malden. "My father was a very quiet man. He never said much. But he always had the nicest things to say about Ted Williams."

Anyway, McLean must have known he had taken a good photo — good enough to run in the *Daily Record*. He probably made a copy for his buddy Keating to run in the *Transcript-Telegram*, along with a copy that he passed on to the *Daily Record* photo desk. It ran the next day — on page three, no less — next to a photo of football star Johnny Unitas posing with two nuns.

On the cutline sheet that's glued to the back of the original, McLean, in his handwriting, tells the story: "Ted Williams with little Ted Athas, 4 years old, of Holyoke, Mass. Ted, with arm around the little fellow, eyes and speaks

to kid to offset latter's expression of awe. Kid all togged out in baseball uniform, sans spikes, top step of Sox dugout."

"No, I wasn't wearing spikes," said Athas, looking at the blowup of the photo that has been in the family's possession for years. "If you look close — real close — you can see that I'm wearing my Howdy Doody sneakers. You can see Howdy's picture on the side of the sneakers."

THAT AIN'T ALL, FOLKS

Ted had his moment with Big Ted, and that should have been the end of it. But at some point during that day's game against the Cleveland Indians — the Indians beat the Sox, 6-4, with Early Wynn besting a fast-fading Mel Parnell — Williams hit a foul ball into the stands that was caught by, you guessed it, Ted Athas.

"I've been going to baseball games my whole life, and that's the only time I ever caught a foul ball," Athas said. "I was the smallest kid in the group, but I guess I wanted it more than the other kids. I scraped myself climbing over the seats and I tore my pants, but I got the baseball."

Little Ted had to fend off some fierce competition to grab the baseball: Among the kids in the group from Holyoke that day was pee-wee catcher Fran Healy, who went on the play nine seasons in the big leagues.

But it was Ted who got the prize, and once again, Keating stepped in. Little Ted's father gave the ball to Keating, who then asked Big Ted if he would autograph it. As he was before the game, when he posed for the picture, Ted was happy to oblige. "To Teddy Athas, best wishes, Ted Williams," he wrote.

Keating, a revered figure in the western Massachusetts sports community, died in 1980. Each year, the Keating Award is presented to the sportswriter who

provides the best coverage of Holyoke's Golden Gloves boxing tournament.

Jim Athas, Ted's father, who cofounded the Holyoke Youth Baseball League with Ron Bennett, passed away in 1999. Even in his last days, the walls of his cellar were filled with mementos from his many years with the Holyoke Youth Baseball League — including his favorite, McLean's photograph of Ted Williams and little four-and-a-half-year-old Teddy.

McLean, a Navy veteran, was a photographer with the Boston *Daily Record*, and later the *Record-American*, for 37 years. He retired in January 1968. "He was so modest," Janet McLean said. "We'd pick up the paper and see that he had taken a great picture of Tony Curtis, and we'd ask, 'Why didn't you tell us you met Tony Curtis?' And he'd just say, 'Well, you didn't ask.' "

McLean passed away in 1986 at the age of 83.

And Teddy Athas?

He grew up to become a shortstop, starring first at Holyoke High School and later at St. Leo's College in Florida. A former teacher, he now works for Lord & Taylor at the Holyoke Mall.

Given everything, you'd think he'd be the biggest Red Sox fan in New England, right?

"I'm a Yankees fan," he said, not even flinching. "I got that from my father. His teams were the Yankees, the football Giants and the Celtics, and, now, those are my teams.

"But Ted Williams was my idol. I wore No. 9 on every team I ever played on. He was the greatest hitter who ever lived, and he was the greatest man I ever met."

PRESS-ING ISSUES

WILLIAMS WAS AT ODDS WITH THE MEDIA

Jack O'Leary

The relationship between Ted Williams and the Boston press was the stuff of legends. But unlike most legends, the depth of their mutual dislike was never exaggerated. "Oh, he was a real son of a bitch," said retired *Herald* columnist Tim Horgan, who covered Williams and the Red Sox for the old *Herald Traveler*. "He had a voice that reverberated through the clubhouse. It would go right through you." Like all reporters who covered the Red Sox of that time, Horgan had his run-ins with Terrible Ted. "It was funny," he said of Williams' postgame demeanor. "If he had a good game, got a couple of hits or whatever, he was unapproachable. He'd tear your head off, but if he went 0 for 4, he was great. He'd talk forever."

The Boston Herald

Sunny, Mild — Temperatures In Lower 70's — Details, Page 2 | VOL. CCXVII, NO. 132 | LATE CITY EDITION | HA 6-3000 | BOSTON, THURSDAY, MAY 12, 1955 | FIVE CENTS | Editorial — Leveling Up The South — Page 16

WEST WARY OF SOVIET PLANS

Ted Back 3 Years To Pay for Divorce

Signs Pact For Red Sox Tomorrow

REDS EVASIVE ON CONTROL OF A-BOMB

Switch of German Unity to Assembly Also Upsets Allies

IKE SAYS TALKS TEST FOR RUSSIA

Boy's Imagination Stirs Sewer Hunt

Watertown Tip On Child False

J.R. Macomber, Financier, Dies

Was President of Mass. Gen. Hospital

The Cost of It All

Beach Project Wins First Test

Adverse Westport Report Overturned

GOP Senators Warn, Lash At President

Today's Herald

'Booby Trap' Blast Intended For Him, Labor Leader Says

Ted Aiming to Do 'Best I Can, But Says He's Not in Condition

2 Young Children Die as Fire Destroys E. Wareham Cottage

OUR EXCLUSIVE KILT JACKET to be worn with Bermuda shorts

Daily Record — Sunrise Edition

WEATHER — SUNNY, COOL. U. S. Report, Page 2 | Vol. 294—No. 111 40 Pages Boston, Tuesday, May 10, 1955 | 5 CENTS | THE RECORD HAS THE LARGEST CIRCULATION IN NEW ENGLAND

WILLIAMS FAILS TO FLY TO JOIN SOX

Ted's Plans Snarled After Miami Divorce

STORY ON PAGE 3

Arrived

Actor Jeff Stone and his French actress bride, Corinne Calvet, married in Tangier, N. Africa, a month ago, as they arrived in New York from Europe yesterday aboard liner United States. Both had been engaged in Europe with show business. Marriage was second for each. (AP Wirephoto)

The Top of the News

Ted to Sign?
Find Tot's Body
N. E. Shots Last

Push Garage Bill
Auto Strike Vote
Big 4 Talk Due
Pass Postal Raise

Daily Record — Home Edition

BRINK JURY SCORE STILL 0

STORY ON PAGE 3

WEATHER — SUNNY, WARMER. U. S. Report, Page 2 | DAILY RECORD | THE RECORD HAS THE LARGEST CIRCULATION IN NEW ENGLAND | Vol. 287—No. 34 56 Pages Boston, Thursday, August 9, 1956 | 5 CENTS | HOME EDITION

TED WILLIAMS FACES YAWKEY

Sox Owner in Hub to Iron Out His Expectorating Slugger

STORY ON BACK PAGE

Saved From Watery Grave By Police

Joyce Newson, 7½-year-old Dorchester girl, of Montpelier rd., unconscious on stretcher carried by MDC and Boston police, after being found nearly drowned on the shore along Dorchester bay, opposite Monticello ave. Police applied oxygen and artificial respiration, before rushing her to Boston City Hospital.

Daily Record — Legal

DAZZLER NO. 13 BONUS COUPON SEE PAGE TWO | DAILY RECORD | Vol. 287—No. 32 44 Pages Boston, Wednesday, August 8, 1956 | 5 CENTS | THE RECORD HAS THE LARGEST CIRCULATION IN NEW ENGLAND | WEATHER: Cloudy, highest in mid 70's. (Complete U. S. Report, Page 2) | LEGAL

Not 1 Brink Juror in 101

STORY ON PAGE 3

TED WILLIAMS FINED $5000

STORY ON BACK PAGE

Splendid Spitter — This saliva salvo cost Ted Williams, Red Sox star, a $5000 fine imposed by Gen. Mgr. Joe Cronin. Williams was en route to bench in 11th inning after first making a two base muff of a fly ball followed by a streaking clutch of another.

Top of The News

Ted Fined $5000
No Brink Juror
Nasser Decision
Shooting, Suicide
Ousted Col. Cries
Ike Prods Bulganin

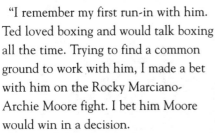

"If he had a good game, he was unapproachable. He'd tear your head off, but if he went 0 for 4, he was great. He'd talk forever."

TIM HORGAN,
RETIRED *HERALD*
COLUMNIST

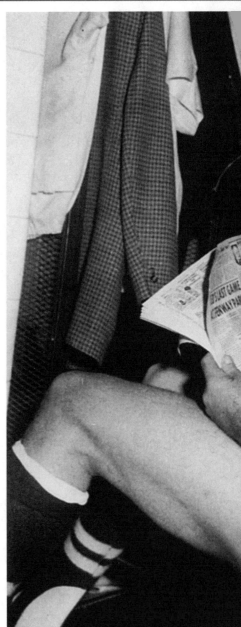

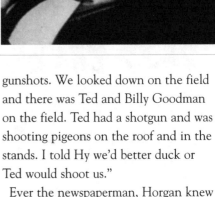

"I remember my first run-in with him. Ted loved boxing and would talk boxing all the time. Trying to find a common ground to work with him, I made a bet with him on the Rocky Marciano-Archie Moore fight. I bet him Moore would win in a decision.

"We made the bet before a game. During the game, I figured the only chance Moore had to win the fight was to knock out Marciano. I wanted to change the bet.

"In the game, Ted had a couple of hits and was in his usual bad mood, only I didn't notice. I just wanted to change the bet. I walked into the clubhouse and marched right over to Ted, and he started yelling for [equipment manager] Johnny Orlando to get me out of there. I was totally embarrassed.

"As I left the clubhouse, [Sox catcher] Sammy White came up to me and said 'Welcome to the big leagues.'"

The press also had its share of fun embarrassing Williams.

"I was at Fenway Park on an off day," recalled Horgan. "Hy Hurwitz and I were in the press box, and we heard gunshots. We looked down on the field and there was Ted and Billy Goodman on the field. Ted had a shotgun and was shooting pigeons on the roof and in the stands. I told Hy we'd better duck or Ted would shoot us."

Ever the newspaperman, Horgan knew a story when he saw one.

"I called the office and told [sports editor] Arthur Siegel what was going on," said Horgan. "He told me he'd handle it. He called the SPCA, and they sent someone right down and gave Ted a ticket for shooting the pigeons.

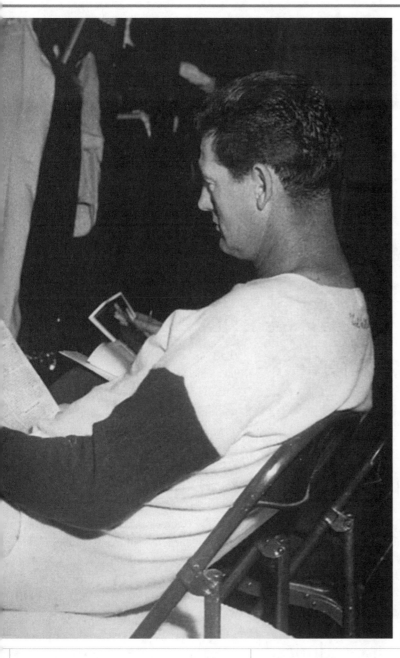

PAPER CHASE: Ted Williams reads the newspaper in the Red Sox Clubhouse on the day of his final game, September 28, 1960.

HERALD FILE PHOTO

of my career," said Horgan. "I still say and will always say I wrote what he said."

One of Williams' Red Sox legacies was his contentious relationship with the media. It filtered down from team to team, era to era. Because of Williams, to be a member of the Red Sox meant being a real jerk with the press.

"He embarrassed you," said Bob Holbrook, who covered the Red Sox for the Boston *Globe* before becoming the American League secretary. "And the younger guys tried to emulate him. He ran the clubhouse, and it wasn't always a very nice place to be."

Still, the knights of the keyboard had a grudging respect for Williams as a player and a presence.

"He was John Wayne," said Holbrook. "He even looked like him. He had that big, booming voice and he had a real presence. You could tell that he came from a tough background. Like a lot of people who came from a poor background, once he got well off, he always ate a lot. Good Lord, could he eat."

For the most part, Holbrook had a good working relationship with Williams.

"I got along with him," Holbrook said, "but then again, I wasn't a columnist. I was just a reporter writing about the games. I think he played the Boston press well. There were so many papers back then and so many guys covering the team.

"He was fine with the out-of-town writers, but I think he did that just to get the Boston guys. He said after he was done playing that he used to put it all on and he wasn't serious.

"Some of it he did put on, but he could lose control as well. He was a big, strong guy and he was scary at times. It was not a pleasure to go in the Red Sox clubhouse."

"He was furious. I wrote the story, but for the only time in my life, I told them not to put my name on the story. I was still going to have to work with the guy, and I never wanted him to know I was the one who turned him in."

Even on the day he was enshrined in baseball's Hall of Fame, Williams was overshadowed by a media clash.

As Williams was about to deliver his enshrinement speech, someone in the crowd yelled, "What would Egan think?" referring to the Colonel, Dave Egan, columnist for the Boston *Record* and

Williams' biggest detractor and tormentor during his career.

Before beginning his speech, Williams muttered what Horgan and Hurwitz reported as an obscenity. The story was given major play the next day.

The story so riled the Red Sox that owner Tom Yawkey summoned Horgan and told him he was sitting close enough to hear what Williams had said and it wasn't an obscenity. Yawkey complained to the *Herald*, which printed a retraction the next day.

"It was the most embarrassing moment

THE OLD MAN AND THE KID

YAWKEY, TED SHARED RAPPORT BUT NOT FRIENDSHIP

Michael Gee

Tom Yawkey was the only owner Ted Williams played for in his entire career. Folklore says the two men had the deepest of friendships until Yawkey's death in 1976. The truth, as usual, is a little more complicated. Yawkey, heir to an immense fortune, loved baseball and admired and truly liked all the players he employed. Naturally, Yawkey adored Williams, the greatest player he would ever have.

Yawkey was as generous to Ted as he could be. The owner insisted Williams be the highest-paid player in the game through the bulk of his career. Yawkey turned an indulgent blind eye to Williams' more—than-occasional boorish outbursts at fans and reporters. The "fines" the Sox levied on Williams were for public relations purposes only and never collected.

Yawkey wanted nothing so much as to be Williams' close friend as well as his employer. Williams did not reciprocate that sentiment.

"I knew he would have liked a stronger relationship with me," Williams once said, "but I never did want to pursue that aspect of it. It was not a father and son relationship."

Williams thought Yawkey was a fine man. He liked him. He never turned down a Yawkey request, long after his playing days were over.

Williams was especially grateful Yawkey sent trainer Jack Fadden to spend the winter of 1951 with Williams, rehabbing the elbow Ted broke running into the outfield wall in the 1950 All-Star Game, a move Williams felt saved his career.

If Yawkey hadn't been the Sox owner, Williams' tempestuous nature would've gotten him traded by 1952 at the earliest.

"I will always sing the praises of Tom Yawkey as a terrific guy and a man," Williams said, and he always did.

But admiration, respect and gratitude do not automatically translate into friendship. There has to be more.

"He was a simple man," Williams said of Yawkey. "He knew how lucky he had been in his life, and he tried to do everything he could to be a good guy. He had an open heart for charity, an open heart for a sad story. He was just a nice, easy man, really and truly."

Aside from having an open heart for charity, everything Williams said about Yawkey was the exact opposite of himself.

SIGN OF THE TIMES: Ted Williams and Red Sox owner Tom Yawkey (right) are all smiles as Williams signs his 1953 contract at Fenway Park after returning from the Korean War.

HERALD FILE PHOTO

Williams felt luck had nothing to do with his life. He seldom tried to be a conventional "good guy." Williams was as complex a person as ever lived in American sports and sure wasn't an "easy" personality.

Opposites do sometimes attract. But read Williams' words more closely, and the truth of his relationship with Yawkey is clear. Deep down, Williams just didn't find Yawkey interesting enough to be his friend.

Williams sought out people who could teach him some new facts about the

world he found so fascinating. His friends came from all walks of life, and they tended to be people who took what they did very seriously, as Williams did, or they were Ted's loyal retainers, a role Yawkey could never play.

Yawkey hunted and fished, but it was social. Williams went out there to catch the damned fish, period.

When Williams played, Tom Yawkey was happiest when drinking, playing cards and shooting the breeze about baseball with like-minded comrades. Life had been good to him, so relax and enjoy.

Williams didn't drink or play cards. No one ever talked more baseball, but not to pass the time of day. Ted Williams idly chatting about hitting was as impossible as Stephen Hawkings idly chatting about physics. And in a long life, Williams never relaxed. That wasn't his idea of living.

Yawkey and Williams shared a time and place. They shared a certain amount of mutual esteem. But to say they shared more than that is another example of legend gilding history's lily.

FAN-NING THE FLAMES

FIERY RELATIONSHIP WITH FANS LEFT WILLIAMS BURNING

Michael Silverman

Ted Williams loved knowing that pitchers could never figure him out. The fact that the fans could drove him nuts. Despite all the cheers that Williams received over his 19-year career, the Hall of Famer could never seem to hear them through the boos. The result was a strained, often ugly relationship with Red Sox fans, one that never fully healed until the latter years of Williams' life. The thin-skinned Williams spit, mocked, made obscene gestures and generally lost his cool on a number of occasions over his career. To some, the worst sin was Williams' refusal, following his rookie season, to tip his cap to the fans. That never mattered to Williams, though. Once the boobirds got under his skin, Williams could never make them go away.

> *"I'm the guy they love to hate. For these 'sports-men,' I can only extend my heartiest contempt."*

SPITTING IMAGE: In one of his most famous exchanges with fans, caught by a *Daily Record* photographer, Ted Williams spits at the fans behind the dugout and in the direction of the press box August 7, 1956, at Fenway Park. He was fined $5,000.

HERALD FILE PHOTO.

SHORT HONEYMOON

When Williams first showed up as a skinny 177-pound rookie right fielder in 1939, he instantly became a fan favorite.

Williams set major-league rookie marks in RBIs (145)/and walks (107) that still stand while slugging 31 home runs and hitting .327. After hitting a home run, Williams would hear cheers when he trotted to right field the next inning. He would lift his cap by the button on top in acknowledgement, a gesture that would increase the volume even more.

Williams would be mobbed by kids after games and often took impromptu trips to Revere Beach with them. He would take them for hot dogs and ice cream, ride the roller coaster, visit the funhouse and earn merit points that should have lasted him his entire career.

Unfortunately, it didn't.

Even in that first summer, Williams, never an incredible fielder to begin with, started to hear it from the crowd when he messed up. In June, after a ball went through his legs and Williams didn't hustle fast enough to retrieve it, the fans got on him.

Williams responded with obscenities.

The war had begun.

OL' RABBIT EARS

In 1940 Williams was moved to left field, in close proximity to the fans, a place where any fan who wanted to could lean over the railing and give Williams an earful without much effort.

This happened often enough to enrage Williams for life.

While his average rose to .344, Williams' power numbers dipped his second year to 23 homers and 113 RBIs. That and too many ground balls between his legs brought out the critics.

Williams responded with more epithets and increasingly petulant behavior. When he didn't run out a hit in September, he took his position in left and between pitches, curled the glove around his mouth to direct insults at the crowd. Articles in the newspapers about Williams' increased surliness coincided with this behavior, and the boos increased as more people

came to the park with the specific purpose of getting on Williams' case.

Writing in the *Saturday Evening Post* in 1954, Williams was blunt about the crowd: "I believe I have the best pair of 'rabbit ears' ever developed in the majors. There might be 30,000 people in the stands, some of them cheering and some of them talking to their neighbors, but if there are a half-dozen giving the old razoo, I can spot them in a matter of seconds. I know who they are before a half-inning is over. A lot of the regulars at Fenway Park make a practice of giving me the business every time they come out to see a game.

"I'm the guy they love to hate. For these 'sports-men,' I can only extend my heartiest contempt."

That year, Williams vowed he would never again tip his cap.

'Never, never will I tip my cap to those damned New England buzzards," he said. "Do the pitchers tip their cap to the crowd when they strike me out?"

Obviously, the atmosphere was being complicated by more than just baseball. Feelings were getting involved, and Williams could never keep the fans from hurting his.

SPIT CITY

Williams certainly had his moments of being treated royally by the fans, particularly when he returned as a war hero in 1946 after missing three seasons.

But it did not take long for the boobirds to come back.

When he was informed by a writer that a university research project showed that booing was a behavior that occurred primarily after World War II, Williams wondered, "Hell, what were they doing prewar? Asking me for a date?"

Williams got off to a slow start in 1950, and a May 11 doubleheader at Fenway against the Tigers did nothing to help the situation.

In the first game, Williams dropped a fly ball and made a gesture to the booing crowd that seemed to acknowledge that he heard them. In the second game, he made sure they got his point.

With the Red Sox up 2-0 in the eighth, the Tigers loaded the bases. A clean single to left by Vic Wertz went through Williams' wickets, however, to clear the bases and make way for the

eventual 5-3 Tigers victory.

As Williams returned to the dugout after the inning, the crescendo of boos was particularly loud. After bowing three times to different sections of Fenway, Williams concluded his act by flipping the bird to everybody.

Before his at-bat, he spat at the fans sitting near the Red Sox dugout.

After the game, Williams said: "I didn't mind the errors, but those damn fans; they can go [expletive deleted] themselves, and you can quote me in all the papers."

The display prompted Sox owner Tom Yawkey to apologize on Williams' behalf.

"Ted's sorry for his impulsive actions on the field yesterday and wishes to apologize to any and all whom he may have offended," Yawkey said.

"The trouble with baseball," Williams said, "is that you've got to be a politician. Always polishing the apple. I'm not that way. I figure I play good baseball and that should be enough."

Williams did tip his hat to the crowd in later years, including when he returned to Fenway as the manager of the Washington Senators in 1969 and again on Ted Williams Day in 1990.

TEMPER, TEMPER

Williams' saliva and temper became news a couple of other times in his career. On Aug. 7, 1956, a full house was at Fenway to see the Yankees. In the 11th inning of a scoreless game, Williams dropped a routine fly ball from Mickey Mantle. Mantle never scored in the inning, which ended with a good Williams catch, but the fans rode Williams as he ran to the dugout. He became enraged and spit at the fans behind the dugout. Then, at the top of the dugout steps, he spit in the direction of the press box before spitting in all directions.

Williams drew a bases-loaded walk in the bottom of the 11th to win the game. After the walk, Williams flung his bat disgustedly and sprinted to the clubhouse. A *Herald* reporter finally chased him down at the Hotel Somerset, where Williams told him from behind a closed door, "I'd spit again at those booing bastards. I just can't help it. You writers are responsible for this

[expletive deleted]. The whole thing."

Williams was fined $5,000.

In an interview with *Sport* magazine a couple of weeks later, Williams bared his soul about his spitting.

"There's 10 percent up there, the baboon type, who's always got his lungs ready to explode ... If someone could tell me what I could do to show my disgust without spitting or making a vulgar gesture which I certainly am not going to do — I would be grateful. I know I 'm not right, spitting, but gee, it's the only thing I can think of doing. I don't want to smile at them. I don't want to wave my hat at them. I don't want to give them a fist job. All I can do is let a big heave, take in a lot of air and go phooey! It's the best way I can relieve my tension, to spit at them, and I am only spitting at 10 percent of them."

The 1958 season also was rough or Williams.

A batting slump prompted another spit job, plus a $250 fine from the American League, which also ordered an apology. Williams did: "I lost my head. Sorry.

Principally, I'm sorry about the $250."

On Sept. 21, Williams flung his bat into the crowd down the first-base line after a weak popup. Seventy-five feet into the crowd, the bat hit 69-year-old Gladys Heffernan above the left eye. Heffernan, the cleaning woman of general manager Joe Cronin, required first aid but was OK. Williams tended to her between innings and later was heard to say he "felt ready to die."

BITTERSWEET END

Williams never did tip his hat after his rookie year, not even after his final game, when he homered in his last at-bat.

A two-minute standing ovation began when Williams was on deck on Sept. 28, 1960. After he homered to the bullpen roof in right, Williams trotted straight to the dugout. Chants of "We want Ted, we want Ted" echoed through Fenway, but Williams, in spite of the urgings of his teammates, did not leave the dugout

to acknowledge the cheers.

After the game, Williams said: "I must say, my stay in Boston has been the most wonderful thing in my life. If I were ever asked what I would do if I had to start my baseball career over again, I'd say I would want to play in Boston for the greatest owner in the game and the greatest fans in America."

Williams did tip his hat to the crowd in later years, including when he returned to Fenway as the manager of the Washington Senators in 1969 and again on Ted Williams Day in 1990.

Williams was once asked about his attitude, and his response goes a long way toward explaining his actions. "The trouble with baseball," Williams said, "is that you've got to be a politician. Always polishing the apple. I'm not that way. I figure I play good baseball and that should be enough." In the end, it was good enough for Williams, no matter what the fans thought.

THANK YOU: After vowing never to tip his hat again, Ted Williams finally acknowledged the Fenway fans in later years.

HERALD FILE PHOTO

FAVORITE

SAN DIEGO

SAN DIEGO — The uniform Don Larsen wore when he pitched his perfect game in the 1956 World Series hangs neatly behind a sheet of heavy glass, along with the important information that Larsen is a proud graduate of Point Loma High School. Professional golf great Craig Stadler (". . . a product of the San Diego

> **"Ted Williams is an icon as a baseball player, but he's also an icon as a native of San Diego."**
>
> BOB BREITBARD

SON

CLINGS TO MEMORY OF ITS HOMETOWN HERO

Steve Buckley

Junior Golf Association") is honored, as is NBA legend Bill Walton ("Led Helix High to CIF Section titles in 1969 and 1970.") Ray Kroc, the late owner of the San Diego Padres and the man who made McDonald's a household name, is remembered sartorially: One of his trademark checkered sports jackets is on display.

FIRST STEPS: Ted Wiliams, who also was a star pitcher in high school, signed his first professional contract with the hometown San Diego Padres, a first-year team in the Pacific Coast League. He didn't hit a home run his first season but hit 23 homers in 1937.

PHOTO COURTESY OF SAN DIEGO HALL OF CHAMPIONS.

But it is somehow understood, as soon as you step inside the San Diego Hall of Champions, a neat, spacious sports attic located in the middle of this city's magnificent Balboa Park, that the star of the show, the clerk of the works, the headliner is . . . Ted Williams.

They don't beat you over the head with it, and, yes, San Diego's many other sports notables are given their various and appropriate moments in the sun, but memories of Ted seem to be everywhere.

Heck, step into the office of Bob Breitbard, who made his fortune running an industrial laundry company and then created the Hall of Champions, and the room is its own tribute to Ted Williams. Sure, Breitbard's office has a signed pair of Bill Walton sneakers, and sure, there are not one, not two, but THREE Tony Gwynn uniforms — a Padres uniform along with baseball and basketball uniforms from Gwynn's days at San Diego State. But it's hard not to notice the Ted bat, the Ted ball and the

autographed picture that reads, "To Bob Breitbard, one of my greatest friends ever . . . Ted Williams."

And do you remember that famous Sunday night television appearance in 1994 when Teddy Ballgame, Larry Bird and Bobby Orr appeared together with WBZ's Bob Lobel? Breitbard has a signed photo of the event hanging in his office, and, no offense, but we suspect it's not there because of Bird and Orr.

"Ted Williams is an icon as a baseball player, but he's also an icon as a native of San Diego," Breitbard said during the

> **They don't beat you over the head with it, and, yes, San Diego's many other sports notables are given their various and appropriate moments in the sun, but memories of Ted seem to be everywhere.**

summer of 2000. "People connect him with Boston, and that's OK, because that's where he became famous. But San Diego is where he grew up."

Breitbard, who followed Williams at San Diego's Hoover High School and would later become one of Teddy Ballgame's closest friends from back home, then got to the heart of the matter: "San Diego is where Ted Williams got his start. And we want to make sure that people never forget that."

THE SAN DIEGO KID

Breitbard was correct in his assessment of the situation. Though New Englanders — even those who never saw Williams play — have long believed the Splendid Splinter to be one of our own, the reality is that we didn't produce him. The Ted Williams who debuted with the Red Sox in 1939, astonishing the world of hardball with a .327 average, 31 home runs and a league-leading 145 RBIs, was already a finished product. He was young and cocky, to be sure, but the raw talent and the great swing were already there — manufactured on the dusty ballfields of

San Diego.

Before Williams ever played for the Red Sox, and before he put up a dazzling 1938 season with the minor-league Minneapolis Millers, he was an original member of the old Pacific Coast League San Diego Padres. And before that, The Kid was a kid from the streets of San Diego whose exploits at Hoover High School made him a local legend even before the big-league scouts knew his name.

"People here identify with him as a great baseball player, but also as a native of San Diego," said Bill Adams, a former executive with the big-league Padres who went on to become executive director of the San Diego Hall of Champions. "I played a little baseball in my day. I graduated from San Diego High School in 1952. And I always knew who Ted Williams was, and that he was from the same city I was from.

"I'd go to the movies and see Ted Williams in the newsreels, and I would say, 'Wow, he's one of us. That's a San Diego guy up there on that screen.' "

Williams was born in 1918, the first of two sons of Sam Williams and his wife, the former May Venzer. The couple had met after Sam's hitch in the U.S. cavalry had ended, and they settled in San

Diego. He ran a small photography shop downtown. Meanwhile, May Williams devoted her days — that is, devoted her LIFE — to her many crusades of behalf of the Salvation Army. Known by neighborhood folk as "Salvation May," she worked feverishly to raise money for her special cause.

As Ed Linn wrote in his book, *Hitter: The Life and Turmoils of Ted Williams*, ". . . Her special mission was ministering to the needs of drunks, prostitutes, and unwed mothers. That's a night beat, of course. And in a Navy town like San Diego, which had a thriving red-light district, there was never any lack of calls on her services."

Sam Williams, moreover, had his own outside interests. He was a man of drink and rarely home. When his photography business failed, he became an inspector of prisons for the state of California, a job that frequently, perhaps conveniently, kept him on the road.

Now, add to this the fact that young Ted Williams' younger brother, Danny, was at first sickly and then later involved in various scrapes with the law, and a picture emerges of a young Theodore Samuel Williams, often on his own as he grew up, trying to put the pieces of his life together and make

HALL OF HONORS: Both of the Most Valuable Player awards that Ted Williams won are showcased in San Diego.

sense of it all.

In the Salvation Army, May Williams found a life. But in baseball, young Ted Williams found salvation. He was five years old when the family moved into a small bungalow at 4121 Utah Street, and the house wasn't far from North Park, which was where young Ted discovered the joys of applying bat to ball. His life would never be the same.

Thanks to baseball — and thanks, too, to various surrogate fathers who kept an eye on him — young Ted would spend

hours hitting . . . and hitting . . . and hitting. It's just about all he did; though certainly a bright child, young Ted was not what you would call bookish. And when he wasn't hitting, he was hunting or fishing on the many undeveloped fields around his neighborhood. Before he was even in high school, Ted Williams was devoting himself to the passions that would follow him through life — baseball and the outdoors.

Hoover High School opened in 1931. It was named in honor of President

Herbert Hoover, who would be pulverized by Franklin Delano Roosevelt in the 1932 election, but what the heck, by then the school already had been named. Hoover High lacked the reputation of the more established and expansive San Diego High School, but Hoover is where Ted wound up. The fledgling Hoover High wasn't far from his house, it was near North Park, and Williams might be able to stand out at a school with less athletic cache.

Excelling as a hitter and to a lesser

> **"People connect him with Boston, and that's OK, because that's where he became famous. But San Diego is where he grew up... San Diego is where Ted Williams got his start. And we want to make sure that people never forget that."**
>
> BOB BREITBARD

extent as a pitcher, Williams was the first great sports star produced by the Hoover High Cardinals. Over the years there would be others — including Ray Boone (father of Bob, grandfather of Bret) and, years later, Dave Morehead, who in 1965 pitched a no-hitter for the Red Sox, but Ted set the standard for all who would follow. He eventually lured big-league scouts to the University Heights/North Park section of San Diego, but the city's new Pacific Coast League team, the Padres, also had inter-

est. One day, they sent shortstop George Myatt over to take a look, and he came away impressed.

"Daddy always talked about seeing Ted Williams that day in a high school game and knowing he'd be one of the great ones," said Gene Myatt, remembering the many stories told by his father, who died in 2000. "He always talked about his swing, how perfect it was."

May Williams, wishing to keep her son at home, had young Ted sign with the Padres. A spare outfielder for the first-

year Padres in 1936, Williams hit .271 in 42 games. In 107 at-bats, he did not hit a home run. The next year, he hit .291 with 23 home runs and 98 RBIs.

"One day, my father was playing short-stop and Ted was in left field," Gene Myatt said. "It was a tight game, late innings, runner on second, something like that. Well, Daddy looked over his shoulder, and there's Ted, standing out there in the outfield, with his glove in his pocket, and he's practicing his swing with an imaginary bat in his hands. My father had to go out

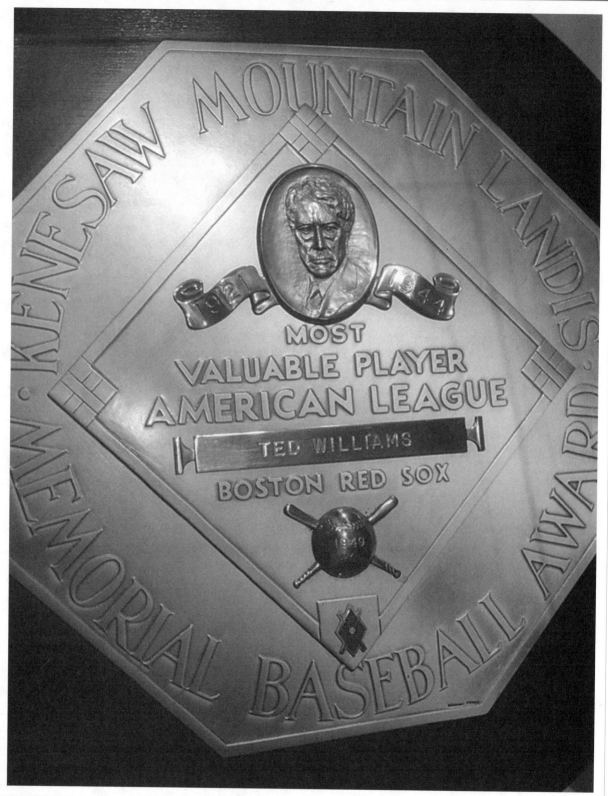

KENESAW MOUNTAIN LANDIS

MOST
VALUABLE PLAYER
AMERICAN LEAGUE
TED WILLIAMS
BOSTON RED SOX
1949

T.W. KENESAW MEMORIAL BASEBALL AWARD·

HALL OF HONOR: Detail of one of the Most Valuable Player awards that Ted Williams won, showcased in San Diego.
HERALD PHOTOS BY BOB GRIESER

there and tell him to knock it off."

It was while the Padres were playing in Portland that Eddie Collins, general manager of the Red Sox, made a scouting trip out West.

"Eddie Collins was looking for infielders," said Johnny Pesky, who would later become a longtime Red Sox teammate of Williams but at the time was a 17-year-old clubhouse boy for the Portland Beavers.

"Bobby Doerr was playing for the Padres that year, and for a while they had his brother Hal, who was a catcher. Eddie was looking at Bobby Doerr and George Myatt."

STAR OF THE WAR: One of the Ted Williams' military honors is on display in San Diego.

HERALD PHOTOS BY BOB GRIESER

Sports fans in San Diego will happily tell you that Ted Williams is the greatest hitter who ever lived.

"My father's knee was bothering him at the time," Gene Myatt said. "Whatever happened, the Red Sox decided not to take a chance on him. They may have come out West to look at Doerr and my father, but they wound up signing Doerr and Ted Williams."

Myatt wound up signing with the New York Giants, for whom he played in 1938 and '39. He also played five seasons with the Washington Senators, retiring with a lifetime .283 batting average.

As for Doerr and Williams, the rest is baseball history. Doerr, a kid from Los Angeles, and Williams, a kid from San Diego, went on to Hall of Fame careers with the Red Sox. And from then on, Ted Williams would forever be identified not with San Diego, but with Boston.

REMEMBERING TED

San Diego never completely let loose of Ted Williams, and he never forgot his hometown. He often returned for visits — some of them official, with press conferences and photo-ops, but sometimes just to get caught up with old friends like Bob Breitbard.

"Bob knows everything about Ted, right down to his shoe size," said Bill Adams of the Hall of Champions. "I think Bob knows more about Ted than Ted knows about Ted."

Williams was on hand when the 1992 All-Star Game was played in San Diego, and he used the occasion to visit the old family homestead at 4121 Utah Street. He also returned to San Diego to be interviewed by ESPN for a documentary, the affair taking place on the Hoover High ballfield, just a few hundred feet from where once stood the diamond on which Williams first commanded attention.

The Ted Williams display at the Hall of Champions minces no words. "A Hoover High graduate and original San Diego Padre in 1936," begins the inscription, and only then does it move on to what Williams accomplished with the Red Sox.

But there is more.

There is a Ted Williams Field at Balboa Park, as well as Ted Williams Field at Hoover High School, with Williams' name emblazoned across the left-field fence in impossible-to-miss red paint. A few years ago, the San Diego Padres built a Ted Williams Little League park at Morley Field.

And if that isn't enough, be aware that the lunch counter at the Hall of Champions features The Ted Williams, which is roast beef with cheddar cheese. (The Bill Walton is a vegetarian special consisting of sprouts, lettuce, tomatoes, avocado and sliced cucumbers.)

Sports fans in San Diego will happily tell you that Ted Williams is the greatest hitter who ever lived. They'll you how he hit .406 in 1941 and that he had a .344 lifetime average and that he hit a dramatic home run in his last time at-bat.

But now and forever, they will tell you first that Ted Williams was from San Diego.

GAME SAVES YOUNG TED

FINDS SOLACE IN HONING SPECIAL SKILLS

Michael O'Connor

The son of a semi-derelict father and a religious zealot mother, Ted Williams endured a lonely, alienated boyhood in San Diego. His father was an increasingly infrequent visitor to the family home and his mother was obsessed with her service to the Salvation Army, even to the exclusion of her children.

While Williams was known as Theodore Samuel Williams, his birth certificate showed that he was actually named Teddy. He later changed it to Theodore on his own by crossing out the Teddy and writing in Theodore in ink. While he had no known relative named Teddy or Theodore, it was assumed he was named after Teddy Roosevelt, whom Williams' father, Sam, claimed to have served under as a Rough Rider. Sam Williams also claimed to have participated in the charge of San Juan Hill.

His mother, May, was of Mexican and French lineage.

Williams had a younger brother, Daniel, who definitely inherited a wild gene but about whom not much was known. And what was known wasn't good. Daniel spent his youth in and out of trouble with the law. He was a known thief and carried a gun.

When Ted came home after a road trip in his first year of professional baseball, he found his car, a 1938 Buick, up on blocks. His brother had stripped all the tires and sold them.

When Williams finally started to make good money after the 1941 season, he completely renovated and enlarged the family house in San Diego. His brother backed a truck up to the house and stole all the new furniture and appliances, including a washing machine and a sewing machine, and sold them. May Williams had her son arrested, and he served a sentence in San Quentin. He later was in the Army but was dishonorably discharged.

After World War II, Dan Williams straightened himself out and became a contract painter and an interior decorator. He later married, had two children and reconciled with Ted.

In 1957, Danny contracted leukemia, and Ted regularly chartered planes to fly him to Salt Lake City for medical treatment. The stress of her younger son battling cancer ruined Williams' mother, who suffered a breakdown. Danny died in March 1960 at 39. May, whom Ted had placed in a nursing home in Santa Barbara, Calif., died the next year.

Ironically, May Williams' neglect may have been a major contributor to Ted's greatness. May would spend many nights tending to the lost souls of drunks and prostitutes, while Ted and Danny would often be locked out of the house.

Worse, Ted might be be dragged along with his zealot mother, who would regularly proselytize from street corners. "Salvation May," in her official uniform and bonnet, tambourine in hand, would approach drunks, prostitutes and unwed mothers. And since San Diego was a classic Navy town, with all the social woes that designation might bring, she always enjoyed a brimming client list.

And if Ted's mother was dedicated to the Salvation Army, her son would be, too. And he was — until baseball turned his head and sent him AWOL. Sunday School conflicted with Sunday morning baseball games at a nearby park, and as far as young Ted was concerned, God would understand. He began to play for both adult (Sunday morning) and youth (afternoon) teams and soon was starring for both.

He was just 14 years old.

In truth, he was not totally neglected by his mother; at least she was around. She bought her son a mitt. When she learned

FAMILY PORTRAIT: Ted Williams (left) poses with his mother, May, and his brother, Daniel, in a photo taken during Ted's early childhood years in the San Diego area.

PHOTO COURTESY OF *THE SPORTING NEWS*

of his hunting passion, she purchased a rifle for him. And when he indicated a tentative interest in tennis, she bought him a racket. Unfortunately, he'd hit a tennis ball so hard, the strings would break. They both agreed it was not his game.

Meanwhile, Ted found refuge in his burgeoning baseball world. Night after night, his mother tending to the world's wounded, he would enter their small, cluttered backyard with his bat and work on his swing for hours in the dark. By age 12, he was already developing a nascent home run swing, concentrating on striking the lower half of the ball with an uppercut motion to gain greater loft.

Williams dreamed of playing in New York's Polo Grounds, because his idol, Bill Terry, played for the Giants, and Terry had hit .400. Even as a youngster, when other kids admired slugger Babe Ruth or hurler Walter Johnson, Williams appreciated just how difficult it was to get a hit almost half the times at bat.

Why was Ted a lefty at the plate? He batted left-handed because of a neighborhood park where he and his young friends played ball.

The park had a short fence in left, and if a batter hit a ball over the short wall, he got fewer points than if he hit the ball over the right-field wall, which stood much

further away. Ted had little trouble hitting the ball long distances from the left side, so he immediately took aim at the wider expanse in right.

Meanwhile, Sam Williams apparently drifted in and out of their lives. Through her Salvation Army duties and charitable works, May Williams met a lot of civic leaders and politicians. When a new governor was elected in 1934, Sam Williams was appointed a state inspector of prisons, and there is little doubt whose influence got him the political plum.

The father's estrangement [at least physically] was now essentially complete. He now worked out of the state capital in Sacramento, hundreds of miles north, and his duties sometimes sent him to San Quentin prison — where son Danny had reportedly done a stretch.

But by 1939, Sam Williams' patron in the governor's office had been turned out by the voters. Mr. and Mrs. Williams were soon divorced. He opened a photo shop and eventually remarried.

With Sam Williams so often out of the picture, his son soon found guidance, maybe even salvation, in a series of surrogate fathers, writes Ed Linn in his book, *Hitter: The Life and Turmoils of Ted Williams*. One was George Lutz, a poultry retailer and

dedicated outdoorsman in his mid-20s, who lived across the street. Lutz introduced Ted to hunting and fishing.

Even as a teenager, Williams had preternatural hand-eye coordination, and he used that gift to become a crack shot and a dead-on fly caster. Lutz would take his protege to San Diego's Crystal Pier and out on the bay, or across the border for all-day hunting trips in Mexico.

Both sports take patience, a quality Williams possessed in limited supply. While he was willing to put in the time required to be a good angler, both in terms of learning to cast and waiting on fish, he was less accepting of inept riflery. If he squeezed off a bad shot, Lutz recalled, young Ted was likely to follow up with a angry barrage of blasts from his gun.

Another mentor was former college and minor-league player Rod Luscomb, also in his 20s, who focused on Williams' already prodigious hitting talent.

All the young player wanted to do was hit baseballs, then hit more of them. That was a dedication Luscomb, who perhaps saw his own fading career continued through his protege, could understand and appreciate.

The two would hit balls all day, for days at a time. In one especially poignant anecdote, Linn recounts how when there was no one around to shag the baseballs, Williams would run home to borrow a coin from his mother and pay a kid to chase them down.

Only later did Luscomb learn that Williams did not go to his mother but rather used his own lunch money to employ the shaggers. The future Splendid Splinter was exposed only when the school nurse suggested to his mother that her son was looking scrawnier than usual and could use a good lunch.

When Williams was selected into the Baseball Hall of Fame decades later, there were two men he singled out for their impact they had on his earliest success in the sport: His high school coach Wofford "Wos" Caldwell and his big brother hitting pal, Rod Luscomb.

WHEN THE KID WAS A KID

Michael O'Connor

Herbert Hoover High School had quite a pitcher in 1936: Ted Williams. The strapping young man was already a good hitter, but coach Wofford "Wos" Caldwell also saw he had talent on the mound — and perhaps he had an early inkling of Ted's haplessness in the field. The coach was smart enough to keep the young player out of right field.

At any rate, Caldwell [whom Ted would later recognize at his Hall of Fame induction] first got a glimpse of the future superstar when he was named coach of the brand new Hoover High, which had opened in 1931. Williams had a sandlot reputation, of course, but Caldwell was skeptical.

Until the Hoover High baseball tryouts of 1934.

It was January, and the playing field was still being used by the football team, so the baseball hopefuls headed for an open patch between buildings. Ted, already confident but still in junior high school, shouted to Caldwell from a stoop, "Coach, let me hit." The Kid was only 15, and Caldwell was concentrating on his upperclassmen, so he ignored him.

Finally, as the tryout session was winding down, the coach was on the mound and motioned the new kid into the box. Williams hit a monstrous fly. Then another. Caldwell stopped pitching and asked the boy's name. "My name is Ted Williams," the batter responded. "I graduate from Horace Mann Junior High on Friday and I'll be here next Monday." He hit several more sky shots for good measure.

Williams, of course, made the team and immediately began to obsess about his weight — or lack thereof. He was still a splinter if not yet the Splendid One. He bemoaned the fact that he had skinny legs and lacked the bulging muscles of his big-league heroes.

High school teammate Les Cassie recalled the duo would have malted milks every day at a soda fountain, located across from Hoover High, as a bulk-up strategy. "Neither of us ever gained a pound," Cassie remarked.

Despite his self doubts about his size, Williams' scientific approach to hitting had him booming balls farther than the muscle boys. One friend recalled how major-leaguer Babe Herman, holding out from the Pittsburgh Pirates, came to town and put on a hitting exhibition, one that

THE GANG'S ALL HERE: A young and gangly Ted Williams (kneeling, far left) poses with his Hoover High teammates and coach Wofford Caldwell.

Williams was on hand for.

"Oh, I wish I had power like that," Williams said wistfully.

Then he got up, stepped into the batter's box — and easily outdistanced Herman's best shots, his father recalled. "I said, 'Ted, you're a doozy.' He never seemed to realize how good he was."

His bat helped Hoover beat bitter crosstown rival San Diego High School as well as every other team in the area, on the way to taking the league title. Ted hit a mere .588. As the No. 2 pitcher, he also won four games.

It wasn't long before Bill Lane, a local sports impresario who hoped to bring professional ball to San Diego, got word of Williams.

Other pro and semipro scouts and their bird dogs were also on the youngster's trail. May Williams made it plain she didn't want her Teddy leaving home just yet, and so when the Pacific Coast League welcomed Lane's new San Diego Padres into the minor league fold, the home team soon sported a new local star.

The Padres were not Williams' baptism into adult baseball; he had played for one of San Diego's many semipro teams for 64 games in his senior year at Hoover. The man who would become baseball's high-est-paid player started out by earning three bucks a game, plus a couple of milk shakes, a hot dog or a hamburger and free transportation to the game.

On the unpleasant side, Williams' "now you see him, now you don't" father started to show up at his games. When Williams graduated, his father appointed himself his son's agent.

Williams was invited to a regional tryout at a local park, but the day before the tryout, he was hit on the thigh by a pitch and could barely run. The tryout was watched by the great Branch Rickey, whose first criteria in judging a player was his running ability. On a good day, Williams wouldn't impress anyone with his speed. On a day when he was hobbled, he didn't have a chance, and Rickey passed.

Before he signed with the Padres, Williams almost signed with the New York Yankees. Bill Essick, the San Diego-area scout for the Yankees, offered Williams $250 a month to sign with New York and report to their Binghamton, N.Y., team in the Class A Eastern League. Williams' contract would have been raised to $500 a month if he made the team. Williams' mother put her foot down; she didn't want her teenage son to move that far away.

So signing with the Padres seemed to be the best way for Williams to gain valuable experience while keeping peace at home.

Three days after he and his Hoover High teammates had lost the state championship to Escondido High, Williams signed his first professional contract with the Padres.

The pact called for $150 a month, and Mrs. Williams was promised they wouldn't trade her son away until after he'd turned 21. And if he was sold to a major-league team, she would receive 10 percent of the purchase price.

Unfortunately, his mother's proselytizing on behalf of the Salvation Army — and, more embarrassing for Ted, the attendant fundraising — soon spread to Padres games.

The young prospect could only watch and wince as his mother pointed him out to anyone and everyone, note that she was his mother, and ask for money for the poor, the forgotten, the unfortunate.

Inevitably, the press soon began to report on her behavior and eccentricities, which hurt Ted deeply. He began to seriously wonder about the wide world beyond Southern California and his difficult family circumstances.

And the poisoned seeds of his relationship with the press began to germinate.

THIS OLD HOUSE

MEMORIES GOOD AND BAD LINGER AT 4121 UTAH STREET

Steve Buckley

SAN DIEGO — Every once in a while — usually during the tourist season, but sometimes on a random weekday in the spring or fall — Terry Higgins will look out the window in his living room and see curious folks looking back at him. Higgins never bothers to ask these people what they want. He knows. He always knows. "They're here to see the house Ted Williams grew up in," Higgins says. "They've read about it, or they've seen something about it on television, or maybe somebody told them about it, and now they want to see for themselves."

HOME OF A LEGEND: Ted Williams' one-story bungalow at 4121 Utah Street in San Diego, located on the edge of the city's University Heights and North Park Neighborhoods.

HERALD PHOTOS BY BOB GREISER

The house of which Terry Higgins speaks is a one-story bungalow, modest yet neat, at 4121 Utah Street in San Diego. Located on the edge of the city's University Heights and North Park neighborhoods, the house has changed very little over the years. Oh, the neighborhood has changed. It's busier and more cluttered than it was in Ted's day, with cookie-cutter apartment complexes having replaced many of the old homes, and former fields of brush have been developed. But to step inside 4121 Utah Street is to step back in time, to Teddy Ballgame's youth.

Though many houses of this type have had their walls torn down to create more wide-open rooms, the rooms at 4121 Utah Street remain small and dark. The kitchen, though updated over the years, is compact. To walk from room to room, one can't help but think: Ted slept in this room . . . Ted ate breakfast in that room . . . This was his mother's room. Walk into the bathroom and you can't help but think: a teenage Ted Williams practiced his swing in the mirror.

Higgins, a retired postal worker, has lived in the house since 1975, when his mother purchased it for $41,000. Eileen Higgins passed away in 1988 and Terry has lived alone in the house since. "It was always a pleasant home to me," Terry Higgins says. " Mom loved it. Now I don't think Ted was too happy here, but I still say the house has good spirits. I've always been happy here, especially when Mom was here. I've had no bad

HOME OF A LEGEND: Ted Williams' one-story bungalow at 4121 Utah Street in San Diego, located on the edge of the city's University Heights and North Park Neighborhoods.

HERALD PHOTOS BY BOB GREISER

feelings about this house."

Higgins recalled a visit made by Ted Williams in 1992, when he was in town for Major League Baseball's All-Star game, which was hosted by the Padres at Jack Murphy Stadium.

"There were cameras and all that," Higgins says. "He seemed glad to be seeing the place again, and he walked around, showing off all the rooms. He was very happy to show the back room,

because he added that one on. He paid to have it built after the 1941 season, when he hit .406.

"I love to tell people about that room," Higgins says. "There's an extra room in my house because Ted Williams hit .406 that year."

According to Higgins, Williams said," My God, it's been so long," as he stood in the living room.

But Higgins also recalled something

Williams said as he was leaving the house. Turning to look back at the living room one last time, the Splendid Splinter remarked to Higgins, "Whatever you do, don't get famous. It's a pain in the neck."

"I think this house has some bitter memories for him," Higgins says. "He was alone a lot as a kid. His father was never around and his mother was doing her activities with the Salvation Army.

INSIDE A LEGEND: An inside look at the modest one-story bungalow in which Ted Williams grew up in San Diego.

HERALD PHOTOS BY BOB GREISER

"I looked out the window one day and saw a TV crew out there. They were nice. I'll look out the window once in a while and see some people pointing. Once every three or four months, someone will ring the doorbell and ask, 'Is this the house Ted Williams used to live in?' "

TERRY HIGGINS,
HOMEOWNER

So I don't think he'd look at this house as a place he'd like to come back to, you know, spend a lot of time. I think when he said that, he was thinking about his youth, and that perhaps some things could have been different for him.

"As for me," Higgins says," I like it here. I like the neighborhood and I like the people. Plus, I'm too lazy to move. And if people are going to come by once in a while to see the house that Ted Williams grew up in, I don't mind a bit.

"I looked out the window one day and saw a TV crew out there. They were nice. I'll look out the window once in a while and see some people pointing. Once every three or four months, someone will ring the doorbell and ask, 'Is this the house Ted Williams used to live in?' "

A few years back, Terry Higgins thought about unloading the house and moving on. But then he thought about

it. Would the new owners welcome the occasional visitors who are curious about Ted Williams' childhood home? Or would they turn these Teddy Ballgame aficionados away?

"I love taking care of the old place," Higgins says." It's my house, but I also know that it'll always be Ted's house, too. Besides, where would I go?"

LEGACY
LIVES AT
HOOVER

Steve Buckley

SAN DIEGO — When Ron Lardizabal took over as head baseball coach at San Diego's Herbert Hoover High School, he faced a problem. Here was a school with a rich sports history, its gymnasium walls plastered with the names of onetime student-athletes who had advanced to the pro ranks, but it troubled him that many of today's students didn't know much — if anything — about those legends of yesteryear. Lardizabal's solution to this dilemma was simple: If you wanted to play baseball at Hoover High, you had to be an expert on the greatest star the school ever produced.

In other words, you had to know your Ted Williams.

"When you think about what Ted Williams meant to baseball, and what he meant to this school, it seemed important to me that the students should know about him," Lardizabal said. "I didn't want them to just know that he played for the Red Sox, or that he's in the Hall of Fame. I wanted them to KNOW Ted Williams."

Along with teaching his young players about the infield-fly rule, turning the double play and hitting the cutoff man, Lardizabal also offered a crash course in Teddy Ballgame 101. And as things evolved, it turned out to be an independent-study course. The coach assigned all incoming players to write an essay on the life of Ted Williams. If they didn't hand in their essay, they didn't play baseball at Hoover High School. No exceptions.

"It gives me tremendous satisfaction to meet with the new players every year and tell them — or remind them — that Ted Williams went to this school," Lardizabal said. "Look, I know this area has changed. This is a different school from the days when Ted Williams was here. The school is mixed now, and there are a lot of immigrants in attendance. It's an inner-city school, with a lot of students who are new to the area.

"But we feel we're on the upswing again. There are a lot of things we want to do in the future, but you can never forget the past. We especially don't want to forget what Ted Williams meant to this school."

Hoover High School, named for President Herbert Hoover, opened in 1931. Although Ted Williams actually lived in the San Diego High School district, his home on 4121 Utah Street was just a few miles from Hoover, and a deal was struck to allow him to be educated (and to play baseball) locally.

Williams became a baseball sensation at Hoover High, even though the short right–field fence at the school's ballfield actually hurt him more than helped him. Because the fence was so close to home plate, balls

"It gives me tremendous satisfaction to meet with the new players every year and tell them — or remind them — that Ted Williams went to this school."

HOOVER'S RON LARDIZABAL
ON SCHOOL'S LEGACY

STANDING ON HALLOWED GROUND: Hoover High baseball coach Ron Lardizabal poses on the field named for the school's most famous graduate, Ted Williams.

HERALD PHOTO BY BOB GRIESER

that sailed over it went into the books as doubles. Williams still managed seven home runs (with a .588 batting average) his junior year at Hoover by doing something he rarely did during his days with the Red Sox: Hitting the ball the other way.

School records do not indicate how many home runs Williams hit his senior year. Nor has Lardizabal been able to determine what uniform number Williams wore during his Hoover years. Even Williams wasn't sure. School officials, along with historians from the San Diego Hall of Champions, keep hoping that, someday, a picture of Williams will surface showing his Hoover High number.

After Williams left Hoover to play professional ball with the hometown San Diego Padres, he returned in February 1937 to receive his high school diploma. Later, as Williams' stature as a big-leaguer grew, Hoover made sure that anyone who entered the school gymnasium knew, at a glance, that this was the place where Teddy Ballgame played his first organized baseball.

The old gym, renovated during the summer of 2000, still has a large-as-life, black-

and-white photograph of Ted Williams hanging on the wall, and homage is paid to other Hoover High sports notables. There's Ray Boone, who adored Ted Williams as a kid and then followed him as a Hoover High star and as a big-league ballplayer. (Ray Boone's son, Bob Boone, was a long-time big-league catcher, and Bob's sons, Bret and Aaron, are current big-leaguers.) Dave Morehead, who pitched a no-hitter for the Red Sox in 1965, is a Hoover grad of a different era, as is Eddie Williams, who made it to the big leagues in the 1980s.

Take an even closer look at the wall of sports stars and you'll see the words to the school's fight song, which read, in part: "Hail Herbert Hoover High, this is our song to thee! Long may our banners be crowned in victory!"

And we are left to wonder: Did Ted Williams sing that song during HIS days with the Hoover High Cardinals?

Outside, the old ballfield where Williams first hit home runs — to left field —is gone. But the new ballfield, neat and compact, makes it clear that this is Teddy's ballyard. "TED WILLIAMS FIELD" scream the letters along the left-field wall, and, yes,

Ted himself once visited the facility and gave it his stamp of approval.

"He did an interview with ESPN when they were doing a documentary on him, and they did it right on the infield," Lardizabal said. "It was a great moment for the school. I was talking baseball with him, and he was using his arms to make a point. He's sitting there in a wheelchair, swinging an imaginary bat. I had my hands out, and he swung into me, and, well, I'm telling you: He was strong as an ox."

Williams also talked baseball with some modern-day Hoover High baseball players.

"We talked hitting — what else?" said Fernando Casas, a 2000 Hoover High graduate who confirmed that, yes, he once wrote an essay on Ted Williams before he ever played a ball game for the Cardinals.

"I talked with him about getting ahold of a fastball," Casas said, "and he waved his hand out in front of him and said, 'If you get a fastball right there, then you take that pitch and knock it right over the fence.

"It was two Hoover High guys talking baseball," Casas said, laughing. "You think I'll ever forget that moment?"

"I wanted to be
the greatest hitter
who ever lived.
A man has
to have goals
and that was mine,
to have people say,
'There goes Ted Williams,
the greatest hitter
who ever lived.' "

-Ted Williams